HAUNTED
NEWPORT
AND THE VALLEYS

South Wales Paranormal Research

First published 2010

The History Press
The Mill, Brimscombe Port
Stroud, Gloucestershire, GL5 2QG
www.thehistorypress.co.uk

Reprinted 2011, 2012

British Library Cataloguing in Publication Data.
A catalogue record for this book is available from the British Library.

ISBN 978 0 7524 5556 3
Typesetting and origination by The History Press
Printed and bound in Great Britain by
Marston Book Services Limited, Didcot

HAUNTED

NEWPORT

AND THE VALLEYS

Contents

Dedication

South Wales Paranormal Research (SWPR) would like to dedicate *Haunted Newport and the Valleys* to a number of SWPR babies that followed in the footsteps of Lolani, who was born in time for our Swansea book, and all put in an appearance ready for Newport! Sam Fitzgerald and Ethan Rees were both born in the summer of 2009, and our editor's very own beautiful daughter, Bethan Elaine Eira Cluer, was born on 17 December 2009 and brought with her a month of snow!

Also we would like to mention Edna Evans, the grandmother of Mark Gulliford, who has himself been heavily involved with this book. Edna sadly passed away in December 2009. She herself had a great interest and belief in the paranormal and is missed by all of her family.

A late addition to the dedication is to congratulate our friends and SWPR colleagues Neil and Kirsten on their Halloween 2009 engagement. Best of luck for a happy future!

Lastly to our friend Simon Hosier – yes, he has finally left, though not to Canada but to China! We hope you come back to visit us soon!

Acknowledgements

I would like to extend my deepest thanks to a number of people who have contributed to the production of *Haunted Newport and the Valleys*, whether through their stories, pictures, interviewing of witnesses, research or editorial support. If it wasn't for these people this book would not exist.

Some of the people who have shared with us their paranormal experiences wish to remain anonymous, and some wish to be known only by their first name, so to the following people and those not listed here (although you know who you are!) I would like to offer my gratitude for your willingness to share your tales: Mark Gulliford, Jill Jeremiah, Rita Richards, Peter Davies, Anne Gatehouse, Marge Smart, Ellen Kershaw, Gareth Francis, Teresa John, Martin, David Hughes, Anthony Adams, Graham White and Kevin Davies. Additional thanks to Mr P.S. Evans of www.oldukphotos.com for providing us with a particularly lovely old photograph of Pontypool Town Hall.

In addition to these contributors, I would like to offer special thanks to a few individuals who have yet again worked above and beyond the call of duty for this project. Firstly to Mark Gulliford who, living in the centre of the geographical area of this book, has worked particularly hard to provide us with a number of stories that are linked to him and his family, and also by providing a number of photographs to accompany these tales. Secondly, extra thanks again to Brian Gent who, through his hard work and contacts, has provided us with some truly unique stories and historical information. Thirdly, thanks to Neil Walden and Ruth Davies, who have spent many days out and about visiting locations, interviewing witnesses, taking pictures and gathering research; we have noted that most of their stories were from pubs! Lastly, thanks again to Richard Rawlings for providing a number of photographs for this book, as he did with the last.

Final thanks go to Graham White, Lesley White, Ant Evans and Keith Whaley who have given their time for proof-reading duties at various stages of the production of this book, a very vital role. Also to my wife Clare Cluer who has, for the third book in a row, been the key figure in pulling everything together ready to send to the publishers, and giving me a regular 'gentle' reminder (nag!) of the deadline – all this while being pregnant and giving birth to our daughter!

For the third and final time, in this book members of SWPR have shown great enthusiasm and dedication towards their passion for sharing the paranormal heritage of Wales with you, the readers. Thank you yet again friends.

Steve Cluer
SWPR Chairman
July 2010

Introduction

www.swpr.co.uk

For the third and final book that SWPR have produced, we would like to begin here with the same quote as in our *Haunted Cardiff and the Valleys* and *Haunted Swansea and Beyond* publications, due to its ability to get right to the core of why we write them. The quote is from *Cambrian Superstitions*, written in 1831 by William Howells who said '... more ghosts and goblins I think were prevalent in Wales than in England or any other country'. As a group we have always believed this statement to be true and, upon researching and interviewing for this book, we now believe it more than ever...

Newport's story goes right the way back to an ancient Celtic settlement over 2,000 years ago, and since this time has seen many changes come its way, including the introduction of a castle when the Normans settled alongside the River Usk in the twelfth century. The remains of this castle can still be seen today as a reminder of its past. Although very little documented evidence remains from this area that shows links with the later Middle Ages, the discovery of a near-complete seagoing vessel in 2002 has indicated that perhaps Newport was a very significant centre of industry at that time.

When we consider the history that surrounds this area and the buildings contained within, it is no wonder that so many people have experienced activity they believe to be an indication of a ghostly presence. In fact, in the city of Newport alone there are over 400 listed buildings, ten historic parks and gardens, sixty-seven scheduled ancient monuments, four archaeologically sensitive areas and 50km² of landscape registered as being of outstanding historic interest. When you add to this the ancient towns of Caerleon, Monmouth, Abergavenny and Usk, the potential for ghosts and hauntings becomes unimaginable.

Again, SWPR members have enjoyed going out to meet with people and discuss their eerie and often frightening accounts, and hope that their efforts succeed in giving you a picture of the experience and feelings it created. In *Haunted Newport and the Valleys* we aim to introduce you, the reader, to a selection of paranormal tales recounted to us by witnesses. Some are from well known and historic landmarks, and some from locations less public, but all are equally active and all are from Newport and its surrounding valleys, often referred to as part of the Newport Marches.

SWPR will be celebrating its seventh birthday in 2010, and looking back over this time we are really very proud that we have managed to complete the three books we set out to produce. It will be an experience we will always look back on fondly despite the challenges it has presented at times. We really hope that you will enjoy the hours spent with this book, and hope that there is something to grab everyone's curiosity and send a shiver up your spine. If anyone has had a paranormal experience of their own, SWPR would love to hear about it as we continue to develop our own paranormal database and attempt to prove William Howells to be correct...

Thank you for taking the time to read our book!
Diolch am fanteisio ar y cyfle i ddarllen ein llyfr!

one

The Fantastic Phantoms of Castles and Historic Locations

When living in Wales there is no shortage of wonderful locations that are brimming with rich culture and history. In fact, considering castles alone, Wales has more per sq. mile than any other country in Europe, from small Welsh strongholds to huge Gothic castles. When we then add the rich Roman heritage of Caerleon, the well-documented Chartist rising and the architecturally beautiful mansions built for high profile families such as the Morgans, we are left with a wealth of information from which to draw. As with many huge and ancient locations, the sheer number of stories they have associated with them meant we could have written whole chapters on some, so we have included a selection of our favourite accounts...

Caldicot Castle, Caldicot

Caldicot Castle is built upon an area that has held great strategic importance for many years. It is documented that the Romans made good use of the area, with Caldicot standing directly on the Via Julia roadway, and the town of Venta Silurum was historically just to the north of Caldicot, and some ruins still remain to this day.

Following the very well-known Norman invasion of 1066, Caldicot was recognised as a location with great advantages and, in 1086, the Normans built a motte and two wooden baileys surrounded by a deep ditch in an effort to keep control of this part of South Wales.

Building work on the stone castle began around 1221, when Humphrey de Bohun, the 'Good Earl' of Hereford, inherited the lordship of Caldicot. His family kept their involvement and control of the castle up until 1373, when the line sadly died out.

In the late 1380s a gentleman named Thomas de Woodstock embarked on a large and expensive rebuilding project within the castle. It was he who ordered the building of the three-tiered Woodstock Tower, the Postern Gate and the Great Gate House.

However soon after, in 1397, Thomas de Woodstock was killed in Calais and the castle then passed down to his daughter, Anne, who went on to marry Edmund, Earl of Stratford. His son, Humphrey, then became the 1st Duke of Buckingham and had control over

The imposing Caldicot Castle.

Caldicot Castle until his death during the Wars of the Roses. Following some further changes of ownership it was then handed over to the Duke of Lancaster, who leased the site to a number of tenants until the mid-nineteenth century when, in 1855, Mr J.R. Cobb purchased the castle. He went on to restore it to much of its earlier beauty and grandeur, and he lived there himself for some time. Caldicot Castle is now owned by the local authority and opens its doors to the public on a daily basis.

The following ghostly tale is that of a young man by the name of Andrew. On this particular occasion, Andrew was at Caldicot Castle to attend one of their well-known and popular medieval banquets for the evening. This was the first time Andrew had ever attended one of these events at the castle, despite having lived in the Caldicot area for some time. He had been persuaded to go on this occasion by his lovely wife. The following tale took place in 2007 and at a time when Andrew knew very little, if anything at all, about the reputed haunting in this amazing building.

During the course of the delightful evening of entertainment, Andrew stepped outside the building to stand just outside by the Great Gate House to smoke a long-awaited cigarette, as smoking is obviously not allowed within the castle itself. One of the huge wooden doors that guard the entrance was standing open and Andrew decided to stand by the open door looking out onto the drawbridge. As he stood there greatly enjoying his smoke, he looked up from the ground and there at the end of the drawbridge he noticed a woman dressed in what he assessed to be medieval clothing; a long, grey gown that reached right down to her feet. She had shoulder-length hair and Andrew guessed that she would be in her late thirties or early forties. She was standing stock still looking up at the castle.

The main entrance to Caldicot Castle, where Andrew saw a ghostly figure.

Because the main door was open, Andrew just assumed that this was probably one of the costumed staff working as part of the banquet evening. More than likely she had gone outside for some air and maybe, like him, a cigarette. He then finished his cigarette and turned to head back inside. When he returned and sat down next to his wife, he mentioned what he saw, joking that even the staff needed to sneak outside for a smoke sometimes, but his wife said to him that she had not seen any staff members that were dressed in grey and that they were all wearing colourful and elaborate costumes.

Soon after, when one of the staff serving at the tables came over to top up the wine glasses, they mentioned the lady in grey to her. She replied that no members of staff would have gone outside because they are not allowed to do so during the event due to them all being very busy. She asked exactly what she looked like, so Andrew described her as best he could. To his amazement, and to his wife's pleasure, she stated that there were definitely no staff working that night who would fit his description.

Thinking he was just having his leg pulled he laughed and said, 'Ok, joke over', convinced that his wife had organised for someone to set him up, but both his wife and the serving lady looked genuinely puzzled at his accusations. Another member of staff came over shortly and he again described the lady he witnessed to her, and this time the reaction was somewhat different. To his surprise, the staff member looked very shocked and a little spooked. She went on to tell them about the story of the grey lady that is thought to haunt the castle and its grounds, and that this spectral lady had been seen by other staff members and members of the public over the years. Did Andrew join the list of those to bear witness to this reputed spirit? He is certainly convinced that he did!

Our second brief tale concerns a visitor to the castle from Canada who was staying with a friend. She wishes to remain anonymous and so for the purpose of the story we shall call her Jayne.

Jayne was visiting Wales for the first time and with her deep love of history was greatly looking forward to spending some time exploring some of the rich heritage of Welsh castles. First on her tour was Caldicot. As she stepped from the car in the visitor car park, she was briefly startled when she heard a loud, deep bang that seemed to shake the ground. Her friend was just climbing from the vehicle and when Jayne asked her what the noise might have been, she said she had not heard anything but that maybe they were doing some kind of re-enactment in the castle grounds, perhaps involving a large cannon she had remembered seeing in the grounds during previous visits. As the pair walked slowly up to the castle entrance, Jayne admired the majestic building and, after paying their entry fee, they walked forward into the inner courtyard and its now grassed area. Immediately they saw the cannon in front of them, but strangely nothing indicating that it had recently been fired. No more than five minutes had passed since the noise Jayne had heard! Asking a nearby visitor who looked like he had been there for some time, they were shocked to be told that no special events were being held that day. Had Jayne heard sounds from a past battle in Caldicot, apparent only to those of us who are able to 'tune' in?

Although we cannot be sure what the noise was, this was not the last strange thing to happen to Jayne that day. In various parts of the castle and grounds she would often turn around to see the owner of the voices she was hearing talking quietly, but on each occasion there was nobody in that direction. Except on one occasion. This time she was sure she saw a small boy in tatty brown clothes – until he seemed to pass through a solid stone wall before her very eyes!

St Briavel's Castle, Tintern

St Briavel's Castle is strictly speaking not quite within the border of Wales. However, due to it being only a footstep away, near the historic and impressive Tintern Abbey, we decided that it would be included due to our own experiences in this wonderful building.

St Briavel's is a Norman castle, originally built as a hunting lodge for King John in 1205 on the site of an earlier stronghold. Its impressive towers were added in 1293. It is now run by the Youth Hostel Association and its warm and welcoming rooms can be stayed in for a very modest fee.

In November 2005, SWPR were asked to help lead a fundraising event overnight for the Cystic Fibrosis Trust at St Briavel's. Although the working team attending that night had been to the castle the previous year, no one could have anticipated the event that kick-started the whole night.

Anthony Adams is a long-term member of SWPR and is very experienced in leading groups during events. Anthony has been described by his colleagues as having the stature of a bouncer and that he wouldn't look out of place playing rugby for the Newport-Gwent Dragons! So not exactly a pushover... at least, not until that particular night.

St Briavel's Castle in its current form.

It was a cold and atmospheric night, with fog drifting around the castle's towers. Not long after arriving and setting up some equipment, the team who would be leading the night took a walk around the castle to familiarise themselves again with the layout and to discuss health and safety issues. One of the towers contains three rooms filled with youth hostel beds, so each room was visited in turn. The ground floor room was inspected first; all there was fine and the team left to climb up to the next floor. The Constable's Room was next, and the team took a good look around, recorded any possible issues, and moved on to scale the stairs up to the top floor and final room. Anthony was the last to leave the Constable's Room.

The rest of the team had made it to the top of the tower and Karen, who is Anthony's sister, noticed that her brother had not caught up with them. She called down the stairs to him, but received no answer. She called again, getting a little concerned. Almost immediately they all heard an enormous bang, like a door slamming, and then scuffling as Anthony appeared running up the stairs! As he got to the top it was obvious to all that he was quite shaken. He explained to the team what had happened.

Anthony says that from the moment that they all entered the Constable's Room he had felt uneasy and eager to leave as soon as possible, but he'd waited while the rest of the group inspected the room. For some reason, regardless of his uneasy feeling, he ended up being the last to leave the room. As he was about to leave to follow his friends and colleagues out and up to the final floor, he felt a strange 'force' rush towards him. Whatever it was, it was so strong that it knocked him off his feet. The door to the Constable's Room then slammed shut in front of him.

'The Castle of St Briavel's', c. 1920.

He scrabbled to his feet and tried to pull open the door, but it would not budge. At the same time the room temperature dropped significantly. Starting to panic a little, Anthony was relieved as he finally managed to wrench the door open, allowing him to catch up with the others.

Upon hearing Anthony's story, the group descended back down to the Constable's Room and not only was the door opening freely, but the temperature had also returned to normal. By now Anthony had composed himself and said he felt absolutely fine – not only in himself, but also about being in that same room.

The tower that hosts the Constable's Room is not without its history. The ground floor room of the tower is aptly named the Oubliette, as in the centre of the room you will find a trapdoor which accesses the original castle's oubliette. An oubliette is basically a dungeon, with its only exit or entrance being a trapdoor or hatch in the ceiling. The name derives from the French word *oublier*, which means 'to forget'; anyone thrown into it never saw the light of day again!

This particular room has had a range of ghostly occurrences during it's time as a youth hostel. The most impressive one concerns a family of four who stayed one night – and they didn't even make it to the morning! During the night the father, who was sleeping on one particular bed in the room, awoke to the suffocating feeling of something or someone pressing down very hard on his chest. Struggling to breathe, he pushed out to try to move whatever or whoever it was away from him, only to find that his hands were finding nothing. He managed to roll out of bed and as soon as his feet touched the wooden floor, the pressure vanished. Petrified to return to his bed, he woke up his wife and children and they left the hostel as quickly as possible.

In the many visits SWPR has made to St Briavel's Castle we have constantly been impressed at the level of activity it yields time and time again, and if you are open-minded enough to take notice of information gained by way of either dowsing or a planchette, much of this activity seems – bizarrely – to relate to the First World War.

Newport Castle, Newport Town

Construction of Newport Castle took place during the mid-fourteenth century. It was built by Hugh d'Audele, Lord of Gwynllwg. The castle served as the administrative centre and the seat of government for the lordship, and it was from here that taxes were collected and justice meted out. The castle has only a modest history compared with other Norman castles, yet has still been owned by many powerful families.

When Hugh d'Audele died in 1347, the lordship and the castle passed to the Stafford family, who retained them until 1521 when the castle and lands were taken by the Crown. In 1547, possession of the castle was granted to William Herbert, later Earl of Pembroke, who chose to lease it to a relative in 1578.

By the mid-eighteenth century the castle had fallen into a largely ruined condition. For the rest of the eighteenth and nineteenth centuries, the castle was in a state of continual decline and was utilised in a variety of ways to satisfy the needs of the growing population of Newport. During the first half of the nineteenth century much of the bailey wall was demolished and removed. In 1820 a brewery was established in the eastern wall buildings, which continued operating until 1899. By 1935 the remaining castle had been placed into the care of the Office of Works, who began conservation work to make the medieval structure safe and remove all traces of work associated with the brewery.

The remains of Newport Castle.

Postcard showing Newport Castle, c. 1980.

Today, the scant remains of Newport Castle can be found in the centre of Newport, nestled by the River Usk. Much of the ruin lies under a road, with only the eastern side of the castle left standing. The surviving wall contains the three towers in which the castle's most important rooms would have been housed. The central tower is by far the most impressive and imposing, and includes a water gate, which would have admitted small boats directly into the castle once the immense portcullis was raised. Above this sits a grand vaulted chamber where Lord d'Audele, amongst others, would no doubt have sat on formal occasions.

A woman called Meg was walking past the castle one time and had a strange experience. It was the top of the central tower to which Meg's eyes were drawn on an ordinary summer's evening. She had recently left work in a nearby bar and was heading towards the city centre to meet friends for a well-earned after-work drink. As she crossed the bridge spanning the River Usk she glanced to the central tower and saw something which should not have been possible: someone walking along the top of the totally inaccessible tower!

Concerned that somehow an individual had scaled the tower, Meg began running towards it, reaching into her handbag for her mobile phone, anticipating that she may need to make an emergency call. She looked up to the tower again, and saw that the figure was still there – fortunately not having fallen or put themselves in any more danger.

Meg called out to a passer-by and exclaimed that there was someone on top of one of the towers in the castle; however, they both looked back up to find that the figure Meg had initially seen had now vanished. The passer-by looked at Meg curiously and said, 'I can't see anyone, it's impossible to get up there, are you sure it wasn't a big bird?' Meg tried to explain to the stranger what she had seen, and that she knew for sure it wasn't a big bird! However, she could see that he did not believe her, and he walked on by.

Confused, Meg walked down to the castle itself to investigate further. It was here that she discovered that it was not even possible to climb up onto any of the three towers; the way was barred by large, heavy iron gates.

Meg was forced to ask herself, if it was impossible for someone to have climbed to the top of the central tower, exactly who or what had she seen?

Tredegar House, West Newport

Set in a breathtaking ninety-acre park, Tredegar House stands proudly as a monument to seventeenth-century architecture. The earliest parts of the building date back to the 1400s and it was home to the rich and powerful Morgan family for many hundreds of years. It was from the mid-1600s that Tredegar House was given a new lease of life with a major rebuild that took almost ten years to complete. However, even before the rebuilding work started it was still suitably impressive, warranting a visit from King Charles I.

However, in 1951 the Morgans left Tredegar House and it took on the role of a school, providing valuable education to the children of the area for over twenty years. The house was then taken over by the council, who started the laborious task of restoring the property to its former glory and splendour.

Ghostly happenings began to be reported in the 1920s, a time when the building was still in use as a house by the Morgans. Servants used to report feelings of unease and a chilling apparition of a lady in white, whose presence was particularly said to be felt on

Tredegar House, West Newport.

the staircase adjoining the Bell's Passage on the ground floor. It seems this ghostly lady was not confined to the house, having also been witnessed a number of times haunting the grounds during the midnight hour.

It was believed that the spectre was Gwyneth Erica Morgan, sister of Evan Morgan, 2ndViscount of Tredegar. Gwyneth tragically died at the young age of twenty-nine, having disappeared in a most mysterious manner. One night, whilst staying in London, Gwyneth simply left the house and was never seen alive again. There is much confusion over the events of that night and of those six months later, when Gwyneth's body was found floating on the surface of the Thames. Even her family's opinion was divided over her untimely departure. Gwyneth's father agreed with the coroner's open verdict, whilst her brother was sure that Gwyneth had sadly committed suicide (the pockets of her clothing were filled with stones). It is even possible that she was murdered, although it is unlikely, especially now, that anyone will ever know for sure.

Gwyneth was not immediately buried at home. It was not until after the death of her father that Gwyneth's remains were reburied with her relatives. Was this the reason she haunted the house? Was there a spiritual longing to be brought home that led Gwyneth to wander the grounds in lonely torment? Even now the white lady is seen by cleaners and staff at the house and is also sometimes heard, singing hauntingly to herself, as she roams the corridors.

Just after the property ceased functioning as a school in the 1970s, Tredegar House underwent restoration and renovation. Whilst this was continuing, a local school was invited to view the progression of the works, an offer taken up with much enthusiasm. Anne was one of the supervising adults during this visit. She was attending a teacher training college and for part of her training she was placed at the St David Lewis School in nearby Bettws. This was the lucky school invited for a special viewing. On this visit, the house was empty except for the three teachers, two classes of children and a guide from the council who would be conducting the tour.

The group had descended to the Bell's Passage, an area of the house that held the bells that would be used to summon servants and staff during its time as the Morgan residence. In the middle of an atmospheric regaling of the history of the property, a sudden loud – and according to Anne, almost violent – ringing bellowed throughout the corridor. Many frightened faces looked up to see one of the servants' bells ringing aggressively and with some force, as if they were being summoned to wait upon a former resident.

The bell that had been rung so very distinctly was just one from the long line of hanging bells. There was no way that it could have been disturbed by any breeze. Indeed, the bells had been originally sited in this location in order to avoid such a possibility. Everyone present was amazed, none more so than the guide from the council who was adamant that they were alone in the house! Upon entering the room that corresponded to the ringing bell, it was found to be completely empty with not a soul in sight.

Most interesting is that this event was witnessed by approximately forty people at the same time, so unlike many ghostly tales it was not just the recollection of a single person that cannot be verified. On further investigation into this eerie occurrence, it was discovered that they had not been rung in fifty years. The use of the bells became redundant when electricity was installed in the house during the 1920s and the wires that operated them were cut. It is true that more recently one of the bells has been restored to

The grounds in which Tredegar House sits.

demonstrate to modern visitors how they might have operated, but on that day in 1974 the wires had been disconnected for some twenty years. How then, did the bell ring on that memorable day? Was this Gwyneth making herself known, trying to attract attention to her mysterious death, or was this some other ghostly spirit playing spooky games?

Anne was to renew her acquaintance with Tredegar House a few years later when she was employed as a research assistant working in the extensive gardens. She was working part-time, conducting market research on behalf of the house regarding its future development. The office for the researchers was situated within the house and she and her companions would often make their way through the building to the nursery rooms and attics. It was always fantastically atmospheric but she had no encounters with the supernatural. Sometimes during that period while she working for the house, Anne would look up at the bells in the Bell's Passage, but they never rang for her again.

However, whilst Anne was working there, a friend's husband took a job as a security man in the gardens. While he was not normally the sort to scare easily, he believes that he encountered the famous white lady in the grounds of the house. Could this have also been Gwyneth visiting the house she and her family loved? The security guard, however, will never know – once was enough for him and he resigned the very next day.

Roman Amphitheatre, Caerleon

The Roman Army's second invasion of Britain happened in AD 43, under the auspices of Emperor Tiberius Claudius Caesar Augustus Germanicus, better known as Claudius I. He was the first Roman Emperor to be born outside of Italy, being born in Lugdunum in Gaul, or modern-day Lyon in France. He ruled Rome from AD 41–AD 54 and his reign came to an end when he was murdered by poisoning.

Roman amphitheatre, Caerleon.

In all some 45,000–50,000 men in four legions, the II Augusta, IX Hispana, XIV Gemina and XX Valeria, together with vast amounts of supplies and ancillary workers, were transported on over 1,000 ships; this fleet alone necessitating the felling of thousands of trees. The command of the invasion was given to Legate Aulus Plautius, who was to become the first Roman governor of Britain. There were around 20,000 Roman troops and about the same amount of auxiliaries; the auxiliaries were very much a part of the Roman Army but the soldiers themselves were not Roman citizens and were recruited from all parts of the empire.

The Roman Army marched into Wales in AD 48 under the command of Publius Ostorius Scapula; he firstly attacked the Deceangti tribe in north-east Wales, who surrendered with little resistance. However, the Silures tribe of south-east Wales and the Ordovices tribe of north-west Wales gave very strong resistance to the Romans and Ostorius Scapula spent several years fighting them. One of the main leaders of the Welsh, or Celts as they were at the time, was a tribal leader called Caratacus, who had fled from the south-east of England when the invading force landed. He was finally defeated in AD 51 when he fled to the Brigantes, but unfortunately he was then handed over to the Romans by their queen! However, the Silures tribe still gave strong resistance to the Romans without their leader.

After the death of the Roman General Ostorius, the Silures won a victory over II Augusta. The further invasion of Wales was put on hold until a Roman general, Caius Suetonius Paulinus, attacked northern Wales and captured Anglesey in around AD 61. The Silures tribe was finally subdued by Sextus Julius Frontinus in AD 78 after a series of campaigns.

Roman Legionary Museum in the centre of Caerleon.

In around AD 75 the II Augusta legion was based in Caerleon in Gwent, known at that time as Isca Augusta. They built a permanent fortress there with barracks, baths and an amphitheatre, all surrounded by a big fortress wall. The fortress was home to between 55,000 and 60,000 soldiers, most of whom were legionaries.

The legionaries would have trained in the amphitheatre, which would have included weapons and battle training and marching. Gladiatorial battles and public executions were also held there for the public to witness and enjoy; therefore it is no surprise that in the amphitheatre there is a shrine to Nemesis, the goddess of vengeance.

The II Augusta was based in Caerleon until AD 300. When the legion left they would have knocked the buildings down, which could have accounted for the start of the demise of Caerleon's Roman buildings and the amphitheatre itself. Even so, Caerleon has one of the best preserved amphitheatres, barracks block, Roman baths and fortress walls in existence. Today you will also find a small museum with all the discoveries from the sites on display.

This story involves two investigators belonging to SWPR. Mark Gulliford and David Hughes had already heard many a ghost story about the Roman remains in Caerleon: marching soldiers, horses, chariots, battle drills – both heard and seen –and visions of ghostly figures wandering amongst the remains, to name but a few.

Back in 2007, Mark and David decided to begin a long-term investigation into the Roman remains in Caerleon, concentrating around the amphitheatre itself. Since then they have witnessed quite a few unusual things…

One particular evening Mark was in the amphitheatre and he very clearly heard a voice directly behind him. Turning to see who was talking to him, he was stunned to find no one there or, in fact, anywhere near him. Mark is convinced that whoever it was that spoke, said 'Sin dex'. Following some extensive research, Mark has discovered that this is Latin for 'left right'!

On another occasion, whilst walking around the amphitheatre arena floor, Mark stopped suddenly upon hearing from behind him the clear stamp of a foot. He described it as if there was someone walking or marching around following him, and whoever it was had suddenly stopped with a final definite stamp.

He and Dave have also been sure they have seen ghostly figures lurking in the doorways leading to the arena floor, but on closer inspection no one could be found. They have also both witnessed strange little lights floating around the arena. Could these shadowy figures possibly be responsible for the sounds Mark had heard?

As both Mark and David had heard the sound of clinking armour, heavy footsteps and voices on a regular basis during their investigations, they decided to start doing some regular EVP recordings. EVP, or Electronic Voice Phenomena, is where a voice recorder – either digital or analogue – is used to record whilst conducting an investigation in the hope of capturing voices or other sounds which are not heard by the human ear during the time of recording.

So far they have had some really interesting recordings. One seemed to sound like someone giving an order or an aggressive battle sound, as you would imagine a Roman legionary would make when thrusting a sword or weapon out. Although the sound was

A sculpture in Caerleon commemorating the town's Roman heritage.

definite, it wasn't clear enough for them to make out what was said. This type of recording became quite common for the pair.

There was one sound, however, that they managed to record on two separate occasions. This was slightly different as Mark and David had decided to try an experiment. Based on the thought that Latin would have been the most common language back in Roman times, they decided to call out in Latin to see if this would get more of a response from any possible ghosts in the amphitheatre. Speaking in Latin, David introduced himself on the tape and then stated that he was from the Silures tribe. Imagine their surprise when, as they listened back to the tapes, there was an additional response to his statement saying clearly in Latin, 'You are'! So far the amphitheatre seems to be the most active area of those they have investigated amongst the Roman ruins in Caerleon. Could the spirits of the legionaries who trained in the arena still be present? Are those failed gladiators who lost during their final battles trying to seek peace? Or is it maybe the tormented souls of those who themselves were tortured and killed during the public executions? David and Mark have promised to continue their investigation in the hope of finding out.

The Shire Hall, Monmouth

The Shire Hall in Monmouth has a long and turbulent history. It was built in 1724 on the site of a sixteenth-century market hall. One hundred years later, it was to become the scene of one of the most significant trials in British history.

The Chartists, with their aspirations of increasing the rights of the working classes through electoral reform, were seen as a serious threat throughout the early part of the nineteenth century. In 1839, authorities in Newport heard rumours that the planned Chartists' protest was actually a ruse; the Chartists were armed and intended to seize the city. Stories circulated along with fear, for if the Chartists were successful in Newport it would encourage others all over Britain to follow their example.

When John Frost, the leader of the Chartist protest, arrived in Newport along with 3,000 marchers, they discovered that the authorities had placed many Chartists under arrest and were holding them in the Westgate Hotel. The Chartists marched to the hotel, chanting 'Surrender our prisoners!' Soldiers had been placed inside the hotel and when given the order, they began firing into the crowd. Twenty were killed and scores more were wounded.

The trial began in the Shire Hall on New Year's Eve 1839. Many Chartists, including John Frost, were tried for treason in this very building and he, along with two others, were found guilty and condemned to death. On 16 January 1840, they were brought from Monmouth Gaol to hear the sentence:

That you, John Frost, and you, Zephaniah Williams, and you, William Jones, be taken hence to the place from whence you came, and be thence drawn on a hurdle to the place of execution, and that each of you be there hanged by the neck until you be dead and that afterwards the head of each of you shall be severed from his body, and the body of each of you, divided into four quarters, shall be disposed of as Her Majesty shall think fit. May Almighty God have mercy upon your souls.

However, the severity of these sentences shocked the public and protests took place across Britain. On 1 February the Prime Minister, Lord Melbourne, announced that rather than being executed the men would be exiled for life. John Frost was sent to Tasmania, where he worked as a clerk and then a school teacher.

Today, nearly 200 years later, the courtrooms remain largely as they were during the days of the Chartists' trials. Employees at the Shire Hall feel that the courtrooms retain a strange atmosphere and many are uncomfortable visiting them alone or at night.

Tony, the former caretaker of the Shire Hall, has had several unnerving experiences. Tony held the role of caretaker for more than ten years, right up until March 2008. His job meant that he would need to be in the hall at various times of the day and night, and as a result he got to know the building better than anyone. Tony definitely believes the Shire Hall to be haunted.

Alarm bells would often mysteriously be triggered throughout the day and night with no explanation. Tony often felt that he was being watched, but could never tell who or what was doing the watching. During the daytime he was often present when frightened guests to the Shire Hall reported similar phenomena, along with cold spots and areas of strong scents found throughout the building.

However, Tony's strangest experience occurred on the central staircase, adjacent to the courtrooms. Alone in the building late one evening in 2006, he stepped out onto the top floor landing area in order to use his mobile phone, as the signal was stronger there than elsewhere in the building. He felt the hairs stand up on the back of his neck as he heard a sound which should not be possible in the otherwise empty building; a door latch click loudly on the landing below.

Monmouth Shire Hall, sadly hidden by scaffold during essential restoration work.

Monnow Bridge, Monmouth, is the sole remaining medieval fortified river bridge in Britain where the gate tower actually stands on the bridge.

Tony turned and, to his amazement, saw the bottom of a diaphanous black cloak reaching just below the knee and a man's legs disappearing behind a pillar! Heart thumping, he raced to investigate, knowing that the building was locked and that he was alone. Tony found no one on the landing. All of the doors were locked and the hall remained as quiet as the grave. There was nowhere the man could have hidden from him so quickly.

Pausing to consider his strange and unnerving experience, Tony realised that despite the stairs being uncarpeted stone, he had heard no footsteps; the mysterious figure that he had seen moved soundlessly. Also, when looking around, the location was not subjected to any dramatic changes in lighting that could account for shadows or any other trick of the light.

Recounting his story years later, Tony remains adamant that he saw the bottom half of a figure. While he could not conclusively say that what he saw was the figure of a judge, he does think that this is likely. Tony knows of other people, such as a relative of one of the town officials, who has reported seeing something very similar. Interestingly, a nearby pub, just across the courtyard, also boasts the ghost of a judge. Maybe it could be the same lingering spirit.

Six months after Tony left his job, the Shire Hall secured National Lottery funding. Much-needed restoration and conservation began in earnest. The multi-million pound project intends to see the building returned to its former glory. When the restoration is complete, Shire Hall will become a centre for the interpretation of the story of Monmouth. It remains to be seen if any future visitors will also experience the mysterious cloaked figure on the stairway or whether the judge himself will return to inspect the restoration – but we certainly hope he does!

The Sessions House, Usk

The Sessions House in Usk is a truly beautiful and extremely atmospheric building that was designed by Thomas Wyatt and first opened its doors in 1877. It was designed to house two identical courtrooms on either side of the building. Sadly, in 1944, one of the courtrooms was destroyed in a fire and rendered useless. However its twin room remained in active service for the administration of justice right up until 1995.

The second courtroom has been left very much in its original design and, with the small and practical addition of electric lights, looks pretty much as it did in 1877, with solid wood benches and seating and the original judge's chair. Towards the rear of the room is the dock, with its staircase leading down below to the long passage that would once have led all the way through into the Usk Gaol that sits next door.

The building was purchased by the town council in 2000 for their own purposes, as a meeting place for local groups and also to let out as office space. During this time, due to its excellent sense of atmosphere the Sessions House has been used for many other purposes, such as a set for television, film and theatre productions, and, as we will read about next, a recent Christmas ghost tour.

These ghost tours are held as part of the Usk Christmas Festival and begin in the Sessions House before heading off into the town, and this next story is relayed in the words of Jill Jeremiah, a local councillor and also a former Mayor of Usk:

> Rita and I joined the last ghost walk of the weekend which was a small group of only seven
> people, including the two leaders. As part of the tour we went down into the tunnel beneath

Postcard of the picturesque Usk High Street.

the courtroom from the dock itself. I myself led the way as I knew where the light switch was and Rita was directly behind with the others following.

As we stood in the entrance end of the tunnel, it was agreed that the light would be switched off and the door closed behind us.

We were all standing in the dark and to try and encourage some activity Mark, the male leader of the tour, said 'If anyone is present would you please make yourselves known to the group'. Silence followed. Mark then said, 'Perhaps let us know by banging on the pipes or some other similar way'.

It was at this point that I became aware of a small green light. It was on the left of the tunnel, and I thought it looked like it was at approximately the same height as the join between the ceiling and the wall at the point where the tunnel is now fully blocked up. I then realised that the small light seemed to be getting longer and resembled a narrow rod of light.

This was when I began thinking 'Am I the only one to see this?', when a voice from the rear said, 'There's a light on the left!' With that, the light seemed to move and became almost a stereotype eerie shape moving forward swiftly! Towards us!

Louise, the female leader of the group, was at the back nearest the door and said, 'I see the light and I think we should get out of here as I feel it may be malevolent', by which time given the speed it was coming, Rita was firmly latched onto my arm and my first thought was to get out quickly as we had been advised.

Bearing in mind I was at the front going down, it meant I was at the rear when leaving and although I do not recall stampeding over the living, I was certainly not the last out and neither was Rita!

We returned intact to the dock, where a kind of relieved hysteria set in for a while, and we were all totally thankful to be out of the tunnel, but strangely none of us seemed particularly frightened by the experience. That said, none of us would venture back down into the tunnel; well, not that evening anyway.

I reported this to the town council the following evening at the monthly meeting and they laughed and joked about it but, when I asked if anyone would go and check the tunnel with me, not one of them would! This incident took place during the Usk Christmas Festival 2007, but this was not the last time a few spirits seemed to pop out and pay a visit during tours!

Steve and Clare, on behalf of SWPR, were asked to run the tours in 2008 and had a wonderful time doing so, in particular getting the opportunity to spend time in such a lovely location, but other than that the tours were fairly quiet from a ghostly point of view. However in 2009 this was not the case...

Due to being heavily pregnant, Clare was unable to participate in the tours this particular year, so Steve was joined by his friend and colleague Dave. This time they were running two tours on the Friday night and then a further two on the Saturday. As the first Friday tour began in the Sessions House, the group walked around the entrance hall and rooms discussing the stories of ghostly goings-on, before heading into the courtroom and later, like Jill in 2007, down into the tunnel below. This was where things became somewhat interesting.

Whilst down in the tunnel, the group talked about EVP and undertook a short experiment in an attempt to capture a spirit voice; to their great surprise, it appears they

The Sessions House, Usk.

did just that! After their experiment they went back up to the courtroom to listen to the recording, expecting very little as all had seemed very quiet, but all of a sudden they were shocked and surprised to hear what was actually a fairly clear female voice, in EVP terms, saying "tis cold out there!' Every member of the tour that night agreed that the voice was there and seemed to be saying the same thing. Even more interestingly, it actually was a very, very cold night! This EVP is without doubt one of the clearest SWPR have captured.

The paranormal fun continued the following night during the second and final tour. The first tour of the night had been fairly quiet in the Sessions House and with numbers for the second tour extremely low, the expectations of Steve and Dave were equally small, despite the great EVP recorded the previous night. However, the night became very interesting after the group returned to the courtroom following the final EVP session of the weekend. They all sat around the large square table between the judge's seating area and the dock. Soon after they sat down, a number of people commented that they thought they could hear a low chattering coming from the corner of the courtroom (behind and to the right from what would have been the judge's perspective), so they continued with their EVP playback while most of the attendees were sure they could hear gentle voices all around them in the room.

The group then decided to spend a little extra time in the room and try to call out for any spirits to respond. Steve called out, and moments later everybody found their heart in their mouth when the door in the corner (front left from the judge's perspective) suddenly slammed shut. Steve decided to go and check the door, just to make sure there wasn't a perfectly reasonable explanation for this incident. He was able to report back to the group that the nature of the door was such that it required some considerable effort to close, and certainly not something that would, for example, shift in a breeze. So he again opened the door and returned to the table – then asked for a similar response from any spirits present.

To everybody's surprise exactly the same thing happened again, while all the time group members could hear murmuring voices from the corners of the room. This time Dave jumped up quickly and headed for the door to see whether he could find any explanation, but just as he rounded a bench to head towards the door, the whole group witnessed him stumble back as if pushed out of the way by some unseen force. Dave felt sure something had moved right through him, causing him to feel as if he had turned icy cold, as if walking into a freezer, and the hairs on the back of his neck had raised right up. If you have ever met Dave, you will have seen that he is a very tall gentleman of some considerable build, and certainly not someone that would be pushed easily!

When he did reach the door he also checked and confirmed, as had Steve before, that the door needed a real tug to pull it shut. After Dave returned to the table, the group experienced this phenomenon one more time, along with further voices, before reluctantly deciding it was time to move the tour on and head for the town centre. What was particularly interesting about both the shutting door and the voices around the room was that they were experienced by everybody in attendance, something which rarely seems to occur.

These are but a few of the strange tales that surround this amazing and historical building in the picturesque town of Usk. To a paranormal group the area is of great interest, especially the Sessions House, which has moved right to the top of our list of places we would like to spend a whole night investigating!

The quaint Norman castle in Usk.

two

Pubs and their Spirits... but not of the Liquid Variety!

ublic houses are one of the favourite haunts (no pun intended!) for many people throughout the UK, and Wales is no exception. In fact, most people will tell you that the one thing every village has, no matter how small, is its own pub. Despite their popularity though, how many of us take the time to think about the history behind the building? Wales has some of the oldest serving pubs in the whole of the UK, including one dating back as far as 1380. Ye Olde Murenger House is Newport's oldest pub, dating back to Tudor times, and this is just one of the pubs our keen investigators have visited to compile this selection of tales...

Skirrid Mountain Inn, Llanvihangel Crucorney

The two stories that follow are both from the beautiful and historic Skirrid Mountain Inn. The first tale relates the experiences of a lady named Teresa John, who told us about a very strange night she spent in the building. Our second story centres on a SWPR member named Gareth, following his experiences at the infamous inn. Strangely, Teresa was also present, although at the time of her own experience she had never heard of SWPR. As told to us, this is Teresa's story:

My first experience at the Skirrid Inn happened about six years ago; this was long before I became a member of SWPR myself. My husband Phil knew of my interest in the paranormal, and as a surprise birthday present for me he had booked a room at the Skirrid Inn. I had no time to prepare for the visit as the night he had booked was the day of my birthday, so I nervously and quickly packed an overnight bag. Thankfully the booking was for a double room so my daughter Ceri, who also has an interest in the paranormal, came along with me.

We arrived on a sunny but cold November afternoon, and we were shown to our room by the landlord. The room was large, with a four-poster bed and an en-suite bathroom that was accessed by a few stairs.

The Skirrid Mountain Inn, Llanvihangel Crucorney, built in 1110.

I had a very limited knowledge of the history of the pub, but I did know that it is supposed to be the oldest pub in Wales. I also knew that, allegedly, the infamous Judge Jeffreys once held court here, and that the en-suite bathroom was exactly where Judge Jeffreys would have sent the condemned prisoner to await his fate. I was already imagining the Judge saying, 'Send him down!'

The landlord had told us that when the pub was empty he would be locking all doors and we would be the only ones in the pub that night, as he lived in a little house across the other side of car park.

As you can imagine, by the time Ceri and I went to bed my mind was working overtime. I have to say the night passed without any real incident and Ceri fell asleep almost at once. I eventually dropped off around 2 a.m.

However, I was awakened about 5 a.m. by someone holding my right hand and squeezing very tightly. I tried to think rationally, and decided I had dreamt it and went back to sleep, but again I felt someone squeezing my right hand very tightly. I did not go back to sleep again and, as I was feeling very nervous by this time, I waited for Ceri to wake before I got out of bed to get washed and dressed in the en-suite bathroom.

This is really where my story starts. By now I was wide awake and thinking rationally, and thinking to myself what a wimp I had been during the previous night, the thought of someone holding my hand seemed quite silly in the cold light of day. However, while I was in the bathroom cleaning my teeth, I could see in the mirror above the sink that the toilet roll on the holder which was on the other side of the room was spinning around and around. It was spinning really quickly and didn't stop until the roll was empty and lying on

A sketched postcard of the 'Tea Garden' at the rear of the Skirrid Mountain Inn.

the floor. I had not been near the toilet roll holder and it was across the other side of the large bathroom, so I could not have knocked it. I was the first person to use the bathroom as Ceri, although awake, was still in bed. I walked over to the toilet area and felt incredibly cold, and a feeling of nausea came over me. 'Don't be silly,' I said to myself, but there really was no explanation for what I had seen. I kept looking for reasons for the holder to spin but I could not find one.

I didn't tell anyone of my experience in the bathroom, not even Ceri, as I felt foolish, but knew in my own mind that I had experienced something I could not explain.

We then dressed, had a lovely breakfast, and made our way home.

About six weeks later I was talking to my niece, Denise, who lives in Cwmbran. She asked me 'What was the name of the pub you stayed in for your birthday? Was it the Skirrid Inn?' I told her it was and she said she would send me a newspaper report that she had seen in her local paper regarding the Skirrid.

Well, a few days later the postman handed me the letter from Denise, and when I read it I was chilled to the bone. I couldn't believe what I was reading. I remembered my stay at the Skirrid Inn and my experience in the bathroom, and I also remembered that I had not spoken of it to anyone.

The article in the newspaper said that a couple had been staying at the Skirrid Inn a few weeks after we had been there. It said that lady believed in the paranormal but the man did not. In fact, the man really thought it was all a load of rubbish.

The article went on to say that while the couple were enjoying a drink in the bar the man made excuses to return to the bedroom for something he had left there. He apparently went into the bathroom and asked for something to happen, saying that if anything did happen it could be explained and said out loud 'Come on and scare me if you can'.

It was at this point he saw the toilet roll holder spinning and the paper falling to the floor! He ran out of the room and the couple did not stay the night. In fact, they couldn't get out of there quick enough.

At this moment, reading the article, I froze to the spot. Had I experienced the same thing as this man?

Maybe I should not have felt so foolish at all on that November morning, and just trusted my own instincts!

Moving on to our second tale from the Skirrid Mountain Inn, let us introduce you to the subject of this tale. His name is Gareth Francis; he is a member of the SWPR Executive Committee and is a believer in the paranormal, although as time goes by he is becoming more rational and logical about his previous experiences. He has worked with SWPR for four years and in that time has experienced many occurrences which have had a logical explanation, but as for the experiences of this night, he cannot explain them, no matter how hard he has tried. He is not a medium or a psychic, although he does tend to sense things psychically every now and then. I suppose you could class him as 'sensitive' to those who have crossed over the great divide.

He does admit to knowing some of the history of the Skirrid Mountain Inn prior to this event, thus making it possible that all that happened to him was in some way on a subconscious level, but he very much doubts it!

It was a cold and damp day, 22 September 2007, and nothing much had happened. It was a normal day before an SWPR event, and he had awoken late and prepared his bag with the usual torches and clipboards in order to be ready for the long night ahead.

He was due to pick up Tracey Ellis, his best friend and fellow Executive Committee member, because as usual he was her chauffeur to paranormal events. Whilst driving they talked about nothing in particular, as close friends do, and listened and sang along with many CDs. After a two-and-a-half hour journey, they eventually arrived at the Skirrid Mountain Inn at about 7 p.m.

The usual routine was followed: team members leading the event set up the experiments ready for the night ahead before the guests began to arrive. At 8 p.m., once all members were at the location, the event leader split them into groups with Gareth and Graham White, SWPR Vice-Chairman and Executive Committee member, leading Group Three. In the group were fellow SWPR members and trained paranormal investigators Lesley White, Anthony Adams, Tara Lane, Dave Hughes and Teresa John.

For those of you who do not know the history of the Skirrid Mountain Inn, it is supposedly one of the most haunted locations in South Wales and also boasts being the oldest inn. The Skirrid once belonged to the Barony of Abergavenny, conferred on Edward Nevyle in around 1530. In 1535, after the death of George Nevyle (3rd Baron of Abergavenny), the ownership of the land was willed to all his successors and remained in the family until 1900.

From its earliest times the Skirrid Mountain Inn was a public meeting house as well as an alehouse, and courts were held within its walls. Between 1100 and 1485, manorial courts would have been staged there, along with Church courts. It is alleged that the first floor was a courtroom, complete with a judge's retiring room.

An old postcard of Abergavenny and the Holy Mountain, in whose shadow sits the Skirrid Mountain Inn.

Although no exact or positive records exist, local legend that passes from generation to generation by word of mouth suggests that upwards of 180 persons were hanged at the Skirrid Inn between the twelfth and seventeenth centuries. The last, as the first, was for sheep stealing in the time of Oliver Cromwell. The hanging cycle had come full circle.

Did the bloody hand of the infamous hanging judge brush the Skirrid? Did the 'Hanging Judge Jeffreys' (1644-1689) sit in judgment in the Skirrid's courtroom? Gareth's eventful night at the Skirrid Inn was about to commence...

It was their group's first activity, which was held in Bedroom 2, and something strange happened the minute the group stepped foot through the door, as all five of them started complaining of headaches (ailments they did not have before entering). Things started getting worse; Tara complained of an invisible heaviness pushing her down onto to the floor and Lesley complained of a pressure on her temples. Gareth and Dave could strangely feel some form of electrical field by the cupboard and trouser press (which is explainable to a degree) and, when approaching from the opposite side of the wardrobe, Dave's ring finger began to twitch uncontrollably. The same thing happened to Anthony when he approached the same electric barrier, but he also complained of a pins and needles sensation in his arm.

By this time Gareth had moved over to the bed area and from his records was standing at ninety degrees to the left of it. Graham then went towards the area where the sensations had taken place and decided to open the wardrobe to see what was inside. This was when things got a lot worse, as according to the others present Gareth went very pale and his eyes became sunken. He remembers feeling very faint and dizzy, and he was having great difficulty breathing – basically, he felt as though he was choking. This was a very interesting phenomenon and, after taking a few minutes to recuperate, the intrepid investigators decided to try again, just to see what happened, and much to their amazement the results were exactly the same.

This had now piqued the interest of everyone in the group and, after another period of five minutes for Gareth to recover, they decided to try opening the doors a third time. This time he decided to sit down and once again when the doors opened, in Tara's expert opinion, 'Gareth went funny!' However, this time a wave of immense fear and hatred washed over him, and at the same time Lesley felt a terrible pressure on her temples yet again and her eyes began to water heavily.

They decided it was time to take a different approach to the bizarre happenings, so Gareth and Lesley, who were affected the most, decided to move onto the landing for a few minutes to get their breath back. Whilst there and unbeknown to them both, Graham once again opened the doors. This time it was slightly different; Gareth felt the same sensation, but less intensely, and an overwhelming feeling of something trying to pull him back into the room.

It was then time to finish the activity which was set up in this room and they moved on and continued carrying out various other experiments, including using a planchette, which is used for automatic writing and glass channelling, a form of Ouija. The planchette was the most interesting as some supposed replies they had from 'a spirit entity' known as Sam stated that he knew who was affecting Gareth in the other room. It alleged that it was one of Judge Jeffreys' soldiers called Cenvydd (the name cannot be verified) who stayed in Bedroom 2 and liked to make people feel unwell.

It was creeping towards the end of the night's activities, but Gareth was not happy to just leave without further investigation into the wardrobe and its effect on him, so the group returned once more to Bedroom 2. They tried using technical equipment that they had brought with them but nothing produced any informative results. So, after a few minutes discussion, they decided to try the experiment again. This time Gareth was sitting on the opposite side of the room, relaxed, and on opening the wardrobe door the same choking experience washed over him; he could not breathe and the colour drained from his cheeks.

Now this is when you are all going to think of him as a fool, as he once again agreed to try the experiment, but this time to try and block out any external stimuli. He agreed to sit with his back to the wardrobe, his eyes closed and with earphones on which were plugged into the television playing music, so he could not see and all he could hear was the awful music which is usually played on early morning television, as by this time it was 2.50 a.m. Thinking that it might be his own subconscious causing him to choke whenever the wardrobe door was opened, they tried again. From fellow group members' reports afterwards, at the same time as Graham opened the wardrobe door he began choking. As for SWPR Lead Investigator Graham, he was and still is an open-minded sceptic who is about as psychic as a brick – but even he could not find a logical explanation for this phenomena and how or why Gareth suffered as he did each time the wardrobe door was opened.

If you ever stay in the Skirrid Mountain Inn, beware the wardrobe in Bedroom 2!

The Coach & Horses, Chepstow

Chepstow is famous for its Norman castle which guards the crossing point of the River Wye, and it remains one of the oldest surviving stone fortifications in Britain. Possibly less well known is the fact that Chepstow was Wales' largest port in medieval times, and for many centuries it was the premier shipbuilding port in the whole of the country. Although the nineteenth century found the shipbuilding trade in decline, even as recently as 1917 Chepstow was designated 'National Shipyard No. 1'. Local legend has it that ships' timbers taken from the Chepstow shipyards were used as the oak beams in building the nearby Coach & Horses, a pub that has been serving the thirsty population of Chepstow for hundreds of years.

In 2001, after thirty years of working as an engineer in the diamond mines of Botswana, Ian returned to his native Wales to take over as licensee of the Coach & Horses. This change of ownership seemed to provoke a spate of paranormal activity and Ian was soon to have his first encounter with the resident ghost.

The Coach & Horses has a very long bar at the front of the building with fireplaces at each end that now have wood-burning stoves installed. Someone obviously enjoys this area of the building, as a spectral figure has been seen here on a number of occasions. When the apparition appears it is usually to be witnessed walking the length of the bar. Sometimes it is no more than a sensation of movement passing nearby, while at other times it is the momentary glimpse of a figure at the periphery of the viewer's vision which immediately disappears on being seen. The apparition has been witnessed not only by Ian but also other family members and staff. All agree that the apparition is female and wears predominantly white clothing; it may be a uniform or, more probably, an apron.

The Coach & Horses, Chepstow.

An old postcard showing 'The Castle and Town, Chepstow'.

The most usual time to experience this spirit seems to be between 6 a.m. and 7 a.m. in the morning, which coincides with the time when the current staff are likely to be preparing breakfast for visitors. The bar itself is empty at this time in the morning and much of the main bar area remains visible from the breakfast room. Often Ian has hurried through from the breakfast room back into the bar having sensed the movement of somebody rushing from one end of the bar to the other. On investigation, there has been nobody present in the area. Ian has even dashed out into the street to check if the movement could be due to traffic or a passer-by glimpsed through the windows, but he has always found a quiet and empty street.

Once Ian was aware of the presence in the pub, his reaction was more surprise than fear. Others have not been so casual about their encounter with the resident ghost. One barmaid, who worked at the Coach & Horses for a number of years, came in early one day to collect her wages. As she moved across the bar she heard footsteps and caught a fleeting glimpse of a white figure. She was convinced that the ghost had followed her into the ladies' toilet, which is situated just behind the most active area near the fireplace on the ground floor. She was a little shocked and very frightened by this unusual incident, as you can well imagine!

Whilst the historic nature of the pub is very much preserved, since 2001 the Coach & Horses gained a few South African flourishes. There are elephants depicted on some of the soft furnishings and it now has an African-styled dining room. At the front of the pub the South African flag flutters alongside the red dragon over Welsh Street. Ian feels that the changes, reflecting his time in Africa, seem to have aroused the curiosity of the ghost because in the first four months after he took over there were as many as thirty sightings. After the initial flurry, the encounters with the ghost have been less frequent. It seems that as is the case in many haunted buildings, it is at times of change that the spirit is most likely to become active.

After six years as landlord of the Coach & Horses, Ian found that there were fewer sightings. Then, in April 2007, the smoking ban was introduced. With smoking banned from inside the building, Ian took the opportunity to redecorate the interior, with new carpets and soft furnishing introduced. To his amazement, the ghost seemed to become more active again, seemingly reinvigorated by the changes to the pub and, for a while, it was again seen very frequently.

So, just who is this ghost? The Coach & Horses is an historic building, and the inn passed from the Morgan family, via the exotically named Hezekiah Pask, to the Price family who owned the premises up to the 1920s.

There are some clues that point to a possible explanation. The path of the apparition suggests a domestic servant forever re-enacting her daily routine, such as tending the fires at either end of the bar and wandering the entire length of the ground floor. The layout of the pub has not always been as we see it today. During Victorian times it is known that the original coaching inn was extended to include the alehouse next door, and the configuration of the ground floor became as it is now. For the first time, someone would be able to walk the length of the building, just as the ghost does to this day.

Recently the Coach & Horses has attracted the attention of a medium who has been able to add some intriguing thoughts. The medium claimed that he believed the presence was indeed that of a servant, and that her duties used to include making breakfast and preparing the downstairs fires. Interestingly, he insisted that she prepared three fires as part of her duties. Today there are just two fireplaces, but further investigation into the Victorian floor plans revealed the existence of a third fireplace near to the current front door, something which could not have been known to the medium. As far as we are aware, this ghostly figure is still known to walk the bar area of the Coach & Horses...

The Rising Sun, Rogerstone

Back at the end of the nineteenth century, the census returns for Rogerstone, near Newport, indicate that the Rising Sun and its neighbouring buildings were all occupied by the local canal men. By this time the Monmouthshire canal, which had been open for around 100 years, had completely transformed the area and Rogerstone had become particularly well known for its own section of the canal where fourteen locks were necessary to enable the barges to rise 168ft within half a mile.

Today the Rising Sun is a very warm and inviting building, set across the road from a nice, relaxing countryside walk that can be enjoyed by the side of the canal; however, the history of the pub can be somewhat confusing. The Rising Sun seems to have been used as a name for the cottages previously on the same site but prior to the establishment of a licensed premises itself, so it is difficult to know at what point the pub was opened. Records suggest that the pub was certainly operational towards the end of the nineteenth century. In the late 1920s the Rising Sun was rebuilt, although comparisons with maps from the time would suggest that the building was re-erected in a slightly different place, in the back garden of the original building. The completion of the new building would have coincided with the period when the competition with the railways was making

The Monmouthshire canal.

it uneconomical to maintain the canals and they were no longer going to play such an important role in the district. However, water has played a part in the recent history of the Rising Sun in a very surprising and mysterious way.

Mary has been working at the Rising Sun pub for over fourteen years now, and she states that some of the other staff are not in any way keen on visiting the cellars. It is for this very reason that some paranormal groups have focused their own investigations on the cellars of the pub and they have been reporting some interesting events, including the phenomena of barrels moving of their own accord. Of course, cellars are rarely very nice. They are usually cold, dark and the least inviting area of any building by far, and this might go some way to explaining why people do not like being there in the first place. In addition to the cellars, in the main bar area there have also been some unexplained happenings. On three occasions there have been wine glasses on the end of the bar that have crashed to the floor and broken when they could not possibly have been touched by anyone, not an uncommon type of activity in haunted pubs. However, it is upstairs in Bedroom 5 that one of the strangest of the recent events occurred.

Mary quite regularly has to stay at the pub overnight in order to be available early the following morning to make breakfast for any guests who may be staying over. One morning in the summer of 2008, she had set her alarm clock for about 5 a.m., but around half an hour before that she was dramatically woken up. She reports that she felt as if a bucket of

The Rising Sun, Rogerstone.

cold water had been poured over her and she was absolutely soaking wet all over. The water seemed to be aimed solely at her and the rest of the room itself remained as dry as a bone. At the time she was staying in a small, single en-suite room and she is certain that there was no one else in there at the time, so she is absolutely convinced that she had not been the victim of a joke. Upon checking, she and others found that the ceiling and the plumbing were all fine and they could find no explanation for the strange event within the room itself. Others were able to act as witnesses to the strange soaking that Mary received from this unknown source as she showed them the drenched dressing gown that she had worn during the night.

So what could possibly be responsible for this bizarre event? Some hauntings involving water have been interpreted as being connected in some way with witch trials. However, there is no reason to suppose that this would be any sort of factor here. Numerous accounts of poltergeist activity also involve liquids appearing as if from nowhere so perhaps this incident is more closely related to this kind of phenomena, especially when considering the moving barrels in the cellar.

There is an interesting case nearby which came to our attention at about the same time as Mary related this story to us. We were told by staff of a pub about twenty miles from Newport (who are far more reticent about being identified) of another, even more elaborate, incident involving the use of water. Here, a man staying the night several years ago awoke to find that his shoes, which he carefully stowed away the night before, had been put back into the centre of the room and filled with water. He was furious and left, still to this day wrongly believing that the staff had in some way played a joke on him. So if you ever have cause to stay overnight in a public house approximately twenty miles from Newport, it may be worth stowing your shoes in a sealed bag, just in case!

Ye Olde Murenger House, Newport Town

Situated in the High Street of Newport, Ye Olde Murenger House is an ancient building, its distinctive name coming from the person responsible for collecting taxes (or murages) for the upkeep of the town walls and defences. Researching the history of the pub is quite difficult as the original Murenger House appears to be a stone structure, latterly connected with the Chartist John Frost, which was demolished in the nineteenth century. However, this earlier Murenger House would have been elsewhere on the High Street. The current Murenger House acquired the name at a later date, although the building itself dates back to the 1530s, if not earlier.

The pub looks strangely out of place among the more modern buildings that surround it today, sandwiched between a cocktail bar and a betting shop. Since the 1970s there have been a couple of refurbishments at the Murenger but these have been effected in a way that has maintained the traditional nature of the pub, preserving the old bay windows with their leaded panes and also the historic ceilings with their unusual plaster mouldings. But perhaps something else is still present from days gone by...

Over the years there has been some talk of hauntings by the ghostly figure of a woman who appears in the top-floor window. Other tales tell of the ghosts of a serving wench and that of an elderly man; yet these have not been experienced by any of the current staff.

Left: *Ye Olde Murenger House, Newport.*

Below: *The sign at Ye Olde Murenger House.*

For a building with a history dating back many hundreds of years, it is surprising to report that the phenomena experienced by the present staff seem to have been of a far more recent vintage, appearing to be not so much from the Middle Ages but from the middle of the twentieth century.

Pat has been at the Murenger for twelve years, and is often working alone in parts of the building outside of the normal opening hours. The encounters Pat has had with the ghosts of the Murenger have largely been in daylight hours and have engendered surprise and mystification rather than fear.

A man with a large, black trilby-style hat and a long, rather old-fashioned, dark coat has been seen at the rear of the bar, heading from the front of the pub towards the back. The appearance was not Victorian, but more the look of someone from the years of the Second World War, and was seen at a time when the pub was actually shut and no one of that (or any other) description could have been in the building. On the third occasion the mysterious man was seen, it was when the pub was open and this time he was witnessed by a second person. The man in the hat was followed into the bar but was found to have mysteriously disappeared.

On another occasion at the start of 2008, a spectral woman from a similar period was encountered by Pat. This time it was in an upstairs room, when no one could have been there. Looking up from her work, Pat witnessed the bottom half of a woman disappearing through a door. Although the sighting was fleeting, Pat clearly saw the pale blue dress that she was wearing and the rather old-fashioned floral design that it had on it. This, and the flat brown shoes, again gave the impression of someone dressed in clothing from the 1940s or early '50s.

The last experience that Pat related was not a visual one, but in some ways is the strangest of them all. One morning about two years ago, Pat had been using the floor buffer to clean and polish the front bar. Although this was before opening time and the pub was closed, as Pat turned the floor polisher off she could hear a noise gradually growing louder. It was the familiar sound of a lively pub! Pat could hear the clatter of glasses, muffled conversation, laughter and the general hubbub of a busy bar. Pat is convinced that this was not the sound of the pub in recent times, but it seemed to be a distant echo of times gone by. From the description there is little to help us date this time-slip. However, even though the noise faded and was gone within seconds, during that time she did distinctly hear the ring of the till. Not the familiar electronic beep of a modern till, this was the sound of an old cash register being rung, something not used at the pub for many years.

The history of the building stretches so far back into the past and could offer more obvious tales of Cavaliers, monks and pale Victorian ladies, so what is intriguing about Pat's experiences is that they all date from just the last century. The Second World War period and immediately after must have held particular significance for the clientele of Ye Olde Murenger House. Perhaps the camaraderie had seen them through those difficult times and now they return to re-live their happy memories once again.

The Tredegar Arms, Bassaleg

Bassaleg stands on the outskirts of Newport. It is a small village clustered around the picturesque eleventh-century church overlooking the banks of the River Ebbw, and next door to the church is the village pub, the Tredegar Arms. It is an old and imposing white building that is not only associated with a grisly story dating back 100 years, but more recently there have been unexplained events and sightings in the pub.

The Tredegar Arms is not only at the centre of the village, but was also at the heart of a major murder story, which was to become known as the Tank Cottage murders. This incident involved the killing of an elderly couple, Charles and Mary Thomas, by one William Butler, on 11 November 1909. The involvement of the Tredegar Arms itself was threefold. Firstly, William Butler was a tiler and an odd-job man, who was often employed to do jobs at the Tredegar Arms. He was known as a somewhat eccentric man as he often wandered aimlessly around the village late at night. Secondly, it was also here that he would spend what little money he earned on drink. Lastly, by a quirk of fate, it was also at the Tredegar Arms, Butler's local, that the inquest into the murder of the Thomas's was to be held. In those days it would not be unusual for the local pub to act as the venue for an inquest, the purpose being to establish how the victims had met their end. In this case the Thomas's had been savagely bludgeoned to death.

One day it was noticed that Butler was seen to be spending extravagantly. He claimed that he had won the money on a horse, but this seemed unlikely, and after searches were conducted he was found to be in possession of incriminating evidence relating to the murder; he had a glazier's diamond glass cutter which had been used to take out a pane of glass to gain entry to the victims' house. Even more damning than this, on closer examination Butler was found to have traces of blood on his clothing and he was immediately put on trial for murder.

The Tredegar Arms, Bassaleg.

Whether these events of over a century ago have any bearing on the experiences people have had at the Tredegar Arms in our current time, it is hard to know. For example, one day one of the ladies who helped out with the cleaning looked up from her work to see an elderly man in a cap walking slowly across the bar. She pressed on with her cleaning, believing that she had seen one of the relatives of the landlady. On reflection she recalled that this could not have been so on that particular day, mainly due to the absence of certain family members, and also the fact that the doors had remained locked from the inside. Plus, when she decided to take a look for the stranger moments after witnessing him, the man was nowhere to be seen, having seemingly disappeared into thin air. Could William Butler have been returning for a last drink in his local?

From the outside of the Tredegar Arms it is possible to see that it has been extended to the right-hand side. The cottage next door, originally built for the sexton of the church, has been incorporated into the original inn. From the inside the join is quite clear, with a fireplace, previously at the end of the building, now in a more central position in the enlarged bar. Evidence of a blocked window can also be seen. In taking on the extra space it could be that the Tredegar Arms may have also inherited another ghost from next door. The legend is that Ernie Puck, a reputed former resident of the cottage, hanged himself and is prone to return to his old house!

The current manager of the pub has found nothing remotely paranormal, but this is not the experience of her predecessors, who witnessed a series of unexplained events over the years. Only some of the events reported recently were in the area of the pub which had originally been Ernie's cottage, and there have been unusual happenings in all areas of the pub. However, it was specifically in the old cottage part of the building that the former manager's wife had an unsettling experience. In the room above the bar, to the right of the building, she saw beneath the door a very distinct blue light which

The churchyard adjoining the Tredegar Arms, Bassaleg.

Bassaleg — the best-kept village on four separate occasions!

dramatically increased in intensity. She was understandably frightened by this, and the pet cat who was with her certainly sensed the presence and was suddenly violently sick!

Every night at closing time, the previous landlord of the Tredegar Arms would extinguish the lights and would then have to cross the darkened bar. While not seeing anything at this time, for some unknown reason he never really liked the downstairs in darkness and he felt that it had an eerie feel to it, even though he knew it was the upstairs where the majority of the reported activity took place.

There was one occasion when the landlord's son believed that he had become entangled in an encounter with Ernie himself! At this time a pool table had been set up in the upstairs of the pub for use by the staff and family. This was in a room where some of the dry stores were kept and uniforms were also stored. Whilst playing pool, the landlord's son suddenly saw a blue light, similar to the one his mother witnessed, growing in intensity in the corner of the room. He had a feeling that an eerie presence was close at hand and he became convinced, as if by some psychic moment, that this blue light was somehow the way the spirit of Ernie manifested itself.

The previous managers have since moved on to a pub in another part of the Welsh borders, and while they have been happy to share their experiences of living and working at the Tredegar Arms, they are pleased to say that they have had nothing untoward happening at their latest pub!

But what about evidence of Ernie Puck having been found hanged in the building which now forms part of the Tredegar Arms? It is difficult to know in which period this event was supposed to have taken place. Records confirm that by the 1860s the Tredegar Arms was in the hands of the Tapp family; twenty years later it was occupied by the Morgan family, and there was no mention of any Pucks there or nearby. While the experiences of the people we spoke to are genuine enough, perhaps the mysterious Ernie is little more than a local legend. However, we do know for certain that there was one hanging associated with the Tredegar Arms. This was on 24 March 1910 when William Butler was led to the gallows at Usk Gaol and duly executed for the Tank Cottage murders.

three

Hauntings in the Workplace

For most of us, the place where we work is more than likely the one place we spend more time than any other – is that not a very scary thought in itself? With this fact in mind, it is little wonder that so many people around the world have experienced something paranormal in nature whilst going about their daily duties as they earn a living. In this chapter we share a selection of the more memorable moments some people have had at work, often in wonderful and very historic buildings with a long heritage of their own and, in one case, even a story concerning a phantom cow!

The Newport Transporter Bridge, Newport

It was back in 1906, as a means of avoiding the particularly high tidal range of the River Usk, that the Newport Transporter Bridge was constructed. For the next eighty years, no matter how high or low the tide, the new bridge was able to provide a safe passage for the people of Newport. Day in, day out, vehicles and foot passengers could be transported high above the river by a gondola suspended in the air from a frame. Far below the shipping could pass untroubled beneath the impressive structure that, even after it closed for ten years in the mid-1980s, remained as a magnificent monument to the industrial development of Newport.

Martin, who at the time of writing is the Bridge Superintendent, started working at the Newport Transporter Bridge over ten years ago. On his first day in the job his new colleagues told him that the bridge 'talks to them' and they get to know all the sounds of the great structure under its various stresses and strains. Martin was dubious of this claim but soon he too got to know every sound that you hear when you are 75m above the river. Car alarms and the sounds of lorries and skips from the nearby waste disposal site carry to the top of the bridge; however, you would not expect to hear the sounds of whistling and footsteps when you are working alone that high above the river.

Martin has seen the bridge reopen in full working order following its enforced closure. Despite the excellent care that the bridge received from its dedicated staff, health and

Newport Transporter Bridge as it is today.

The old drill in the Transporter Bridge workshops.

safety considerations later dictated that the bridge should close for a short period while funding was sought to safeguard its future. While this has meant that the bridge has been out of operation, there is a least one visitor who still seemed to enjoy Martin's company, both in the workshops and on the bridge.

As the bridge approached its centenary the Stephenson Street workshops on the eastern side of the river received a complete rebuild. It seemed that whatever ghostly presence might have been present in the workshops was a little suspicious of change. Tools in the workshop went missing, there was a reported incident of a bucket flying across the room to dash itself against the new workshop walls, and the large Denbigh drill that had worked so well since installation in 1906 now refused to work in its new surroundings.

Interesting as these happenings are, it is the events up aloft that are really most remarkable. Over the years, Martin has often found himself working high up on the bridge alone, although this is something that is less common now that there are stricter health and safety considerations. Often, when up high on the bridge, he would sense a presence behind him but would see nothing when he turned around. Less frequently, probably on three or four occasions, he heard whistling and faint footsteps and afterwards could smell the distinctive aroma of pipe tobacco. He has radioed down, only to be assured that he was the only one on the bridge at that time. When up at the summit of the structure, Martin would be at the top of an exhausting 300-step climb and there is no way that the sounds could be carried so distinctly from the river below, and the slightly fragrant smell of the smoke would surely

The Transporter Bridge, Newport, c. 1910.

have dispersed in the unlikely event of it having emanated from the deck of a passing ship. Martin has looked for rational explanations but has failed to find anything plausible. The whistling could not be attributed to the wind in the cables, and besides it was always heard on summer days when there had been little or no wind. In each case the whistling has been a tuneful rendition of a song, albeit one that he did not recognise.

Other workmates of Martin's are also aware of the ghostly presence, which they know as 'Old Joe'. There is no direct evidence to link these phenomena to Joe, who was someone who worked on the bridge for over forty years, but everyone seems comfortable with the idea that it might be his kindly influence.

It also seems that Joe is near to hand in times of crisis. On one night, not so long ago, one of the main winding cables of the bridge broke and needed urgent attention. Martin was in the travelling basket, which was high above the gondola on the bridge and clearly visible to other team members below. Martin's radio sprang to life – it was from the Motor House down below wanting to know who was up there with him. From the ground they could clearly see a second man near to Martin, illuminated in the big halogen lamps of the bridge. The second figure was too distant for them to recognise but he was either walking across or possibly inspecting the huge girder-like boom. Martin confirmed back to the Motor House that he was alone. On that occasion, Martin did not witness anything himself but others felt sure that they had seen Old Joe giving the benefit of his expertise.

Martin feels strongly that what he has experienced could be the presence of a predecessor in his job, maybe an engineer or construction worker from earlier in the twentieth century. Perhaps this worker from an earlier age is just taking a break on a summer's day and possibly admiring the view far below. Whatever the source of the sounds and smells, the feeling that it creates is never frightening; in fact, it makes Martin feel as if someone may be looking out for him and is certainly still looking after the bridge.

The Abergavenny Chronicle, Abergavenny

The *Abergavenny Chronicle* was founded in 1871 by Edwin Morgan, an enterprising local businessman, when it cost just one old penny! At this time the *Chronicle* was based at premises in Frogmore Street, but like most country newspapers was partially printed elsewhere. Much of the news in the paper at this time was national or international, with only the front and back pages containing local news and advertising. In this way the *Chronicle* was able to supply local people, many of whom rarely saw a national newspaper, with up-to-date news and information about issues as wide ranging as fashion and technological innovation.

In 1960, Stanley Straker and his son, John, with their respective wives, took over the running of the newspaper until its sale in 1965, when it became part of the Worcester-based company Berrows Newspapers Ltd and moved to new premises in Cross Street. In the early 1980s, Berrows itself was taken over by Reed International and the *Abergavenny Chronicle* was bought by Tindle Newspapers Ltd, an independent company based in Farnham, Surrey, in September 1983.

Under the ownership of Sir Ray Tindle, the *Abergavenny Chronicle* has gone from strength to strength and in 1996 celebrated its first 125 years by moving from Cross Street to its present premises in Nevill Street, just a few doors away from the building where Edwin Morgan launched his first newspaper almost 150 years ago.

The Abergavenny Chronicle.

The building dates from Elizabethan times, as does the whole street, and it abuts the old town wall. It is comprised of three stories, with attics and cellars, although means of access to the cellars is presently unknown. The façade was revamped in Georgian times, and the original shutters are still in place. A local historian, Frank Olden, has visited the premises and looked in the attic, and reported that the original timber was still present. In the 1800s the building was used as a brewery and some time later it became a fruit shop. It is known that a Belgian refugee dressmaker lived there after the First World War and that it was a family home after the Second World War, before being bought by the *Abergavenny Chronicle* in 1996. So we can see that the building has been lived or worked in for a great many years.

Since the building has been owned by the *Chronicle*, the staff who work there have found the atmosphere in the old building to be quite pleasant. At times though, different members of staff have had odd experiences, ones which should not normally occur in a working environment. They have heard strange noises; for instance, footsteps coming downstairs when there was nobody upstairs at the time; they have noticed the aroma of fruit, oranges in particular, when there are none present; they have heard crashes above them on the second floor; and when going to investigate, the people working on that floor have denied all knowledge.

Liz Davies, the paper's editor, has probably had the most experiences which she cannot explain. For example, one time, on entering the kitchen which was previously clean and tidy, she found sugar had mysteriously been sprinkled around the worktops, with no sign of the packet or bowl. On closer inspection, both the packet and bowl were still in the cupboard!

The ruins of the Great Hall, Abergavenny Castle.

The recently restored motte at Abergavenny Castle.

About eight or nine years ago, she was in the office towards the middle of the building on the ground floor. It was lunchtime and she was sitting in there alone when she suddenly heard footsteps coming down the front staircase. Thinking it was a member of staff going out to visit the local shop for some lunch, she went out to speak to them, but to her surprise found no one there or anywhere near.

Another morning soon after that, Liz was on the first floor having arrived early when she heard someone crying and sobbing downstairs. Rather alarmed, she quickly went down the front stairs and found no one in sight. She went into the reception area to ask the receptionist, but no one had been heard or seen!

One very stormy night in 2005, around 10.30 p.m., Liz and the former editor, Pat, were in the main newsroom accompanied by the IT technician who was investigating a fault with one of the computers. Liz and Pat were standing watching the technician at work. Suddenly Liz felt a pressure on her back like a hand on the top of her shoulder and, turning to speak to Pat, realised that she was no longer behind her but on the other side of the room, something which really sent shivers up Liz's spine.

The most bizarre phenomenon relates to the desk in her office. The first significant occurrence was in the spring of 2005, when electricians were in the building doing work in the offices. When she came in to work on a Monday morning, she found that strangely her desk had been moved. On asking the electricians she found that they had not been in over the weekend, so this was rather difficult to explain. The second experience was six months later. She got up from her desk and stood in the doorway to speak to someone from the editorial staff for about ten minutes. When she went back in, to her surprise, she found that her desk had moved almost 1ft towards the window. No one else shared her office or had entered it while she was away from her desk – it was quite inexplicable.

She was so taken aback that she showed three or four colleagues, took photos of it and even dragged the managing director down to see it for himself. The desk was pushed back into place and the working day carried on as usual. Later that day, Liz left her office and visited the ladies. When she came back she was utterly amazed to find that it had moved yet again!

What could be causing the desk to move? Could it be connected with any natural occurrence like minor earthquakes, even though none had been reported at the time that these movements took place? Could a previous occupant of the building have taken a dislike to the desk and was showing their displeasure by effecting its placement? Or could the alleged presence actually dislike Liz being in the office and was trying to make its feelings known?

University of Wales, Newport – Caerleon Campus, Caerleon

The Monmouthshire Training College, based in Caerleon, opened in October 1914 and over the next fifty years it acquired a national reputation, and due to this success it started to expand dramatically. Fortunately, the college had been built on a large site which allowed expansion around the original imposing building with its distinctive clock tower. Like so many educational institutions, over the remaining years of the twentieth century the college was subjected to various mergers. In 1996 the college became the University of Wales College, Newport, and in 2003 it was renamed the University of Wales, Newport.

The historic clock tower on the Caerleon Campus of the University of Wales, Newport.

As it expanded, there were increasingly rumours that a Roman burial ground had been built over by the new educational buildings. There even began the usual talk of the spirits of Roman centurions marching through various parts of the campus. There have been many occasions when both staff and students have reported hearing sounds that would seem to indicate marching soldiers and large groups of men chatting to themselves, but never any sightings to match these noises.

In 1992 the Caerleon Campus was ravaged by fire. Large areas of the roof were lost in the disaster, revealing very charred rafters, but fortunately the landmark clock tower was left unscathed. However, despite the damage, the fire did not rid the site of the ghostly Romans nor indeed its most celebrated presence, that of a 6ft tall matron who is said to walk the corridors of the university!

The spectre of matron Bertha Ramsey is said to be a familiar sight to staff at the Caerleon Campus, having plunged to her death after toppling over a banister on the second floor back in January 1962. Since her death, there have been numerous sightings of her ghost roaming the corridors near her room on the ground floor. She is usually described as a woman wearing a brown overall with her hair pulled back in a tight bun, and her visits are said to be a well-known phenomenon among security staff who patrol the campus at night.

Some of the university staff have felt themselves being pushed and many claim to have heard strange noises. Several of the security staff have also heard other strange sounds at night and sometimes, in the early hours of the morning, the lift seems to operate by itself, and they watch as the doors slowly open to reveal that there is no one inside. Could Bertha be making an effort to make her presence known to them?

The story of Bertha was covered by the BBC in 2003, when one or two of the staff shared their stories and a small book on the subject of the hauntings was produced. During recent contact while researching this book, some of the security staff and the lecturers were asked to relate any experiences that might indicate that Bertha continues to make her presence felt at the site. Of particular interest are the latest reports from the security team, as they are the people who know the building best and are also there late at night, when the building is at its quietest.

A recent story concerns one of the security men, who tells us that while he was out and about on his rounds he saw what he describes as 'a golden glowing figure'. Interestingly, this sighting was at night and was in the newer and usually less active part of the building. Has Bertha been investigating the new expansions for the college perhaps? This phenomenon does not fit in easily with Bertha's normal activities, and even less so with those of the marching Roman legionnaires – could this be a third haunting for this historic campus?

Another more recent incident does seem to conform to Bertha's traditional activities. This took place in the daytime and in the older part of the building. A carpenter was working with a member of the college team to hang a new portrait in one of the corridors. The atmosphere was described as quiet and there was no one else around at the time. The painting that the two men were hanging was a heavy commemorative photograph and no sooner was the picture in position than it started to move! Not slowly swinging to one side, but rocking uncontrollably! Such was the violence of the swinging portrait that it was impossible that it could be caused by somebody brushing past. Surely this was set in motion by an unseen, mischievous hand? Both men were so scared that they quickly left the corridor.

Later on they tried to rationalise what they had earlier experienced, but to this day remain puzzled as to just what could explain the sight they had witnessed. Could this have been Bertha expressing her views about the person in the portrait, or perhaps she was just trying to let people know she is still around, keeping an eye on the place?

Apparently Bertha was equally mysterious in life and, after her death, there is a story of the campus being visited unexpectedly by her twin sister. Bertha had neglected to mention that she even had a twin, and seeing Bertha alive again (for that is how it must have looked to the people who witnessed the event) must have given some of her old colleagues a nasty fright! Maybe Bertha is still causing moments of confusion and consternation at the college some forty years on, enjoying the reaction.

The Metropole, Abertillery

The Metropole Cultural and Conference Centre is situated in the centre of Abertillery. The original theatre was built in 1892 by a local entrepreneur named Charles John Seabourne, who was thought to have been around twenty years old at the time. Mr Seabourne hailed from Six Bells, a village a few miles away, and was a familiar, if rather clichéd, figure in the area. He sported a handlebar moustache and was often seen to be smoking a large cigar. He owned the Metropole – sometimes in partnership with others – right up until 1952, when he sold it to the local council. Although the date of his death is unclear, it is known that he had two sisters who survived him and who lived in Llanhilleth, again only a few miles away from Abertillery.

The date of the building of the Metropole Theatre coincided with the rapid growth in coal mining in the South Wales valleys, and by the 1920s the population of Abertillery was around 40,000, which made it the second largest town in Monmouthshire, after Newport. The original Victorian building housed a 400-seat theatre, a market hall and a ballroom, but over the years the coal mining industry degenerated in the vicinity and the town's prosperity also slowly declined, impacting on this glorious building. The Metropole itself fell into disrepair and eventually had to close due to structural problems, which included the removal of a central cast-iron pillar which supported the middle of the roof. In 1998 the local museum took over the ground floor to use as a storage area for artefacts; maintaining a constant temperature for the preservation of these items probably helped to prevent the building above falling further into disrepair. However, by 1999 the building was almost in a state of collapse, and this was not to change until 2005, when a £1.4 million grant was obtained to refurbish it and make it again into a multi-purpose cultural and conference centre for the community of Abertillery and the surrounding population.

The rebuilt facility retains a great deal of the original features from its time as a Victorian theatre and music hall, including the ornamental cast-iron balcony and stage. The old ceiling has also been removed to reveal Canadian pine beams, which have been incorporated into the design. In the main auditorium there is seating for an audience of up to 200 people, and the Metropole now hosts events, conferences and exhibitions for regional and national visitors, as well as presentations and performances by local community groups.

SWPR investigator Mark Gulliford looking for evidence in the allegedly haunted corridor.

Ever since the building work began in 2005, and during the period that it has been in use since, there have been a number of strange experiences which can only be described as paranormal. Suzanne Allen, the manager of the Met, as it has become known, describes a number of personal experiences, as well as a strange report from one of the fitters who was very often on site during the period of extensive refurbishment.

One day in October 2005 some contractors were expected to arrive during the afternoon to set a screen up, but they arrived somewhat late at around 7 p.m. One of the fitters went into the corridor between the reception door and the door leading to the stairwell at the back of the building, where the toilets are situated, and upon returning reported that he could smell cigar smoke. Suzanne then entered the same area and was amazed that she too could smell it. However, there was no source for this smell, so none of them could understand where it was coming from. This has occurred another three times in that same area in the stairwell, and also once in the auditorium one early evening. She was told by one of the builders around this time of an experience in the auditorium that appears to link closely to this inexplicable aroma. He was standing on the stage when he suddenly felt very cold, smelled cigar smoke and heard footsteps walking across the floor of the auditorium and in front of the stage. There being no sign of an owner of these footsteps, he left the area much quicker than he had arrived! In addition to this gentleman's experience of this phenomenon, Suzanne has also heard footsteps walking past the front of the stage two or three times over the last year, yet there has never been anyone there. This has again usually occurred in the early evening.

At the other end of the day, a number of Suzanne's experiences have occurred when opening up first thing in the morning. In spring 2007, she opened the Met at around 7 a.m. in preparation for a big conference, and was walking along the corridor that runs from the side of the stage towards the cellar end of the bar area. Having just passed the doors into the auditorium, she heard a loud cough or exclamation immediately behind her. Upon turning around she found she was alone; the sound had been so loud that she went to the reception area to see if anyone was there, but found it empty.

The auditorium of the Metropole Cultural and Conference Centre.

A number of times she has also found the kettle in the bar to be boiling or very warm to the touch. This is very odd as although the kettle is always left plugged in, the cleaner always turns the switch off before leaving at closing up time. Another time when Suzanne was in the bar area she heard a crash in the cellar, which is situated behind the bar. She quickly went into the cellar where she found some plates, which had been carefully left at the back of a worktop, on the floor. Even stranger, as she turned to leave the cellar she found a piece of cake wedged on the handle of the cellar door!

One of the Metropole's other employees, Susan Smale, has also had some personal experiences. From January 2006 to June 2007, this occurred at least once a week when she was the first to be in the building in the morning. She too smelt strong cigar or pipe smoke in the corridor where the toilets are situated, even though this has always been a non-smoking area. Once in February 2006, like Suzanne, Susan also found the kettle in the bar area to be hot even though it was switched off. There were also small puddles of water on the floor in front of the bar door; the water had run from the bar door to under the carpet – a distance of about 1m. Even though she made a thorough search, there was nothing on the bar or above on the ceiling that could have caused the water to be there.

Another employee, Paul Selway, was also subject to some strange experiences. In June 2008, Paul had locked up one night at 7 p.m. and was the first person to open up the next morning at 8.30 a.m. He too found the kettle in the bar area boiling hot, but not switched on. This also occurred on two other occasions, both when opening in the morning.

Paul also experienced more unique occurrences in the bar. At about 10.30 a.m. one morning, he was in the seating area of the bar whilst two other people were in the auditorium setting up equipment on the stage for a concert. Suddenly he could hear 'old'-style singing in the cellar. It lasted for about two minutes; he had not heard the music before at any other time, and it was not being sung by the two people in the auditorium!

The bar area at the Met.

Another unusual experience he had in the bar area concerned a cheesecake. He had placed it carefully on top of the microwave one day and later that day, during a lunchtime buffet, it suddenly seemed to fly off by itself!

One other rather strange occurrence was when Paul took £60 out of the float to purchase some items for the Met and, on his return, he put a receipt in. The next time the cash box was inspected, however, the float was back to its original amount, even though neither he nor anyone else had put any money back in.

Following these experiences that none of the staff could explain, SWPR were invited to conduct an investigation in the Met. Following their usual protocols, they deployed their equipment and conducted a series of six carefully controlled investigations. The most interesting phenomenon recorded – which was corroborated evidence – was the instance when footsteps were heard by the team when in the auditorium. These were heard to pass along the bar corridor and then appeared to be up in the balcony over the bar itself; they continued to be heard for up to three minutes. No one was seen to be causing the footsteps and, therefore, there was no obvious explanation.

Some more very interesting phenomena occurred in the top corridor. While two team members were standing at one end of the corridor, they heard footsteps towards the other end which were repeated on request, and they also heard knocking in reply to knocks that they made. These appeared to genuinely be a form of interaction between the team members and an unknown entity – a real rarity during a paranormal investigation. In the absence of any other obvious cause, the team had to conclude that this was highly likely to be a paranormal phenomenon.

So who is the cigar smoker still walking the boards and corridors of the Metropole Theatre? And why do they have such a fascination with the kettle – and with cakes?

Private Farm, Monmouth

The house at the heart of this story is situated about two miles from the centre of Monmouth. The building had originally been designed by George Vaughan Maddox, a builder who was very active in Monmouth in the 1830s. The house was originally built for Thomas Dyke, a grocer who had become the Mayor of Monmouth in 1832. Later the house was the home of Alexander Rolls, who was the Deputy Lieutenant of Monmouth and part of the famous Monmouth Rolls family which co-founded the motor and aero-engine manufacturing company. After Alexander's bankruptcy and death, the house was to change hands several times. By the mid-1950s the house and grounds were operating as a farm, the owner having a small herd of about twenty cows. It was about this time that Pat started working at the farm.

Pat still lives in the Monmouth area and although all of the following incidents which happened to her are now over fifty years ago, such was their impact that she remembers them as vividly as if it were yesterday. It was back at this time, when Pat was studying at university and was temporarily living close to the main farmhouse (as it had by now become) in a flat around the rear of the property, that she came to believe that the farmhouse itself could well be haunted. It became almost normal for lights to turn on and off, for the keys to turn and the latches to lift, although all were untouched by human hands.

One of the most striking incidents which took place during Pat's time at the farm was one evening when she was returning home from the cinema with a friend and was walking up the long drive to the house. The electric lights, so carefully extinguished before

A view of Monmouth from the hills above.

General View of Monmouth.

Postcard view of Monmouth, c. 1909.

they left, were now all blazing out as if someone was at home. When the farmer was told about the lights he made little of it, saying that it was probably just caused by faulty wiring. However, at other times the owners would admit to suspicions that, just as Pat believed, the house was in fact haunted.

The strangest event related by Pat concerns the animals themselves, in particular the cows that were kept on the farm. There were a couple of strange incidents, one of which occurred on a misty winter's morning. One of Pat's duties was to help with the milking and that, of course, involved an early start. The herd consisted of Red Polls, which are easily recognised by the deep red colour of their coat and their light-coloured noses. The name 'Polls' comes from the fact that the cattle are all naturally 'polled', meaning they have no horns. It was about 6.30 a.m. on this particular morning when Pat and a friend went out to move the cows ready for milking. As was often the case, some of the cows were asleep and one of the first jobs was to quickly go around and gently shove any slumbering cows to move them into the milking area. To Pat's astonishment she went to slap a cow on the rump and her hand passed right through it and, before her eyes, the cow simply vanished! Of course she was absolutely astounded and to this day can think of no explanation for what she experienced.

Pat's story is indeed a strange one, even more so as it is a story of a placid beast. There are similar stories documented elsewhere, but most involving phantom animals in this region refer to the creatures as fearsome beasts. For example, the horses pulling phantom stagecoaches are invariably described as 'wild-eyed', and there are several phantom black dogs thought to be seen in this area of Wales. These are invariably described as 'hell hounds', such as the one that is thought to be the inspiration for *The Hound of the Baskervilles*, associated with Baskerville Hall in Hay-on-Wye. But rarely are there stories of more placid beasts, such as the phantom cow haunting the farmyard to the north of Monmouth.

The Old Exchange, Newport Town

It is hard to believe in this modern age of electronics that, until fairly recent times, many telephone connections were made manually. This involved shifts of operators sat in front of manual switchboards twenty-four hours a day, seven days a week, for twelve months of the year. A telephone exchange is therefore inevitably a place where drama, extreme emotions and tragedy are played out both on the lines of the telephone system and sometimes in the exchange building itself. A new, fully automatic system has now replaced the old telephone exchange in Newport; however, as with many old and historic workplaces, the Old Exchange has had its fair share of paranormal activity. Perhaps its location in a part of Newport that has seen many epic historical events also has something to do with it.

Firstly there was the very lifelike apparition of a man dressed in overalls that was often seen walking in the dimly lit corridors behind the frames which hold the telephone equipment that link in to the network. He appeared to be searching for something on the back of the equipment, as though looking for a fault. Perhaps this same apparition was also responsible for some of the other activity at the exchange. On the night shift, staff often reported hearing doors opening and shutting in the building, yet all those on duty were able to be accounted for. It is important to point out at this stage that, because of their nature, telephone exchanges are very secure buildings and therefore access or egress is controlled at all times.

There have been many similar tales from people regarding one particular room in the exchange. They reported hearing the door at the end of the outside corridor open and shut, followed by the distinct sound of footsteps walking down the corridor past the door of this room. A door to another room further down the corridor was then said to have opened and closed of its own accord. Those brave enough to investigate these incidents have found nobody either in the corridor or in any of the rooms leading off from it. As there was no other way out of either the corridor or any of the rooms, where did the phantom footsteps go?

In the early hours of one Sunday morning, an engineer was carrying out some urgent work on some equipment that had broken down in one of the switch rooms. He was merrily working away, minding his own business, when all of a sudden he heard firm banging on the window behind him. He quickly turned around and, to his horror, was confronted with the sight of angry faces at the window and hands banging it with both fists and clubs! It was then he noticed that the atmosphere and ambience of the room had changed dramatically and become really quite electric. After the initial shock, he pulled himself together and began to look for what he thought was some high voltage electrical fault causing the effect, completely forgetting the apparition he had just seen at the window. Failing to find any source for the obvious electrical activity, he was drawn back to the window, which now seemed to have a strange and mysterious shimmering heat haze in front of it.

Eventually, he summoned up enough courage to cross to the window and look out. Although it was dark and misty he could just make out an angry mob with banners milling outside. The mist seemed to swirl and he was once again looking at the empty street he would have expected to see from that location. Being a Newport boy, he realised

The Old Exchange, Newport town centre.

immediately that he had just somehow witnessed a scene from the Chartist riots that occurred near that location some 150 years before!

Apparitions from further back in history have also been witnessed in the basement of the exchange. One night a monk-like figure was seen to glide through the outer wall, and another operator on a break from her duties reported a semi-transparent woman in medieval dress moving slowly along the corridor. Incidentally, both may have been heading for Newport Castle, which lies not far away from the building in that direction.

A retired employee at the exchange claimed that the most intriguing phenomena at the Old Exchange were the high number of ghost calls reported by subscribers and received within the exchange itself. It seems that for many years, residents of Newport had been harassed by strange, late night telephone calls, many of which had been traced as coming from inside the exchange itself! A thorough undercover investigation revealed that the calls had been made using a line out that had not been used since the Second World War, and had actually been disconnected from the whole network. In fact, most of the reports of phantom telephone calls were traced to disconnected numbers that were theoretically incapable of using the network. As all calls were routed through the exchange switchboard and thus disconnected there, was the source of this phenomena in the exchange itself? The investigations then turned to the nature and content of the calls.

Instrumental Transcommunication (ITC) is the modern name for strange voices that are said to manifest themselves on electronic or electromagnetic transmission equipment.

Old postcard of Newport High Street, c. 1950.

These days EVP is probably the most well-known subcategory of ITC. EVP refers to strange voices that are said to make themselves heard on audio-recording equipment, yet such effects have been around for a lot longer on the telephone. At the Newport manual exchange they had many reports from subscribers of unwanted callers with inappropriate language, suggestive comments and 'heavy breathing'. Over the years they set up a dedicated position on the switchboard with the specific objective of monitoring such incoming lines. The operator would trace the calls to the originating phone line and liaise with the police to enable them to take action and hopefully catch the offender.

One operator tasked with these duties claimed that they now believe some of the voices heard during monitoring were ITC phenomena. Investigation found positive evidence that nominated phones were either not in use at the time of the alleged calls or not even connected. There was even one case when a woman received a short telephone message from her dead son! The family were, of course, outraged that someone should play such a cruel trick; however, once again the telephone from which the call was made had been disconnected many years before. So whether it is in the exchange itself or the lines that passed through it, the old Newport exchange is certainly a most haunted place. Perhaps the removal of that human factor in the new automatic exchange will also remove the paranormal entities?

four

Personal and Private Phenomena

For a great many years we have heard tales of ghosts and hauntings in castles and mansion houses, but we do not as often hear of the experiences many people have in their own home. There are some exceptions of course, including the very well-documented poltergeist in Enfield that has resulted in numerous books and television programmes, but there are far more people experiencing these phenomena and their stories do not get told. In this chapter we would like to bring you a selection of accounts that have baffled and terrified many people at home.

Maindee Estate, Newport

The incidents began several years ago in a typical semi-detached house in a suburb of Newport, named after the Maindee Estate that covered this area before the city expanded in the late nineteenth century. When we talk of the term 'poltergeist', many of us usually recall several modern films where these phenomena have been portrayed in a very frightening and malevolent way. However, the word actually originates from the German translation for a 'noisy ghost'. The physical activity usually associated with these phenomena include mysterious bangs, crashes, furniture moving and the sound of breaking glass, although sometimes nothing appears to have been disturbed. The term also applies to furniture and objects that seem to move of their own volition. This can take on a more sinister tone when such objects are propelled at speed through the air, across rooms, often hitting unsuspecting observers. The term can also be applied to unseen hands that shove, pinch and slap the victim, and in the most extreme cases inflict visible injuries, though it is important to note that cases like these are very rare indeed. Perhaps it is the menacing effects produced by such activity that makes us more aware of such incidents than other tamer paranormal experiences.

Often a poltergeist appears to focus its attention on a single person in the household, usually a young female, and often referred to as the 'agent'. Recent research seems to indicate that, in fact, such activity is far more prevalent around disturbed adolescents, and

The Maindee area of Newport, 1900s.

researchers claim that perhaps repressed fear and guilt in such subjects with hysterical tendencies could somehow be converted into externalised energy forces. Most of the time apparitions do not accompany the poltergeist activity, but in some examples both voices and visual effects subsequently occur. The following incidents, as you will clearly see, have all the ingredients for a classic poltergeist occurrence. At the present time, the mother and daughter involved still live in the same house in which the incidents occurred, and therefore we will withhold their names for the sake of anonymity.

The occupant of the house was a hard-working mother in a single parent family, and she had lived in this suburban semi-detached house in a quiet street for several years. At the time the activities began, her daughter was a teenager and just embarking on that period of her life where the conflicts of study, peer pressure and sexual awareness all began to have an effect on her. The string of events began with a series of strange, unrelated bangs and crashes around the house. A friend suggested that they had experienced similar noises and traced it to trapped air in the central heating system. The mother duly called in a central heating company to investigate and although there was indeed air in the system, they claimed that it should not have resulted in the noises described. Where possible, the engineer also checked the pipe runs to ensure clearance and eliminate noise caused by the expansion and contraction of the pipes.

Despite all of this action, the noises still occurred sporadically, and after a few weeks they began to increase in both frequency and intensity. It appeared that whatever was causing these bangs and crashes was not getting the family's full and undivided attention, and so it escalated the phenomena in an attempt to do so. Next came the unobserved movement of furniture and ornaments, usually at night or when the house was empty. The occupants of the house were beginning to get used to the idea that they had an unwelcome and invisible visitor in their home when the daughter was awoken one night by a scratching sound in her bedroom. Turning on the light, she was terrified to see a book moving slowly along the dressing table to the edge, where it then fell with a deep thud onto the floor. Awoken by her screams, the mother rushed to her daughter's room, but on this occasion she was too late to see the unexplained phenomenon that had just occurred. Not totally believing her daughter, she put it down to a bad dream resulting from a discussion they had had earlier regarding the spooky activity they were currently experiencing in their home.

A week later another incident occurred which confirmed to the girl that, without doubt, their house was indeed haunted. She was awoken this time by something clearly and firmly tugging at her hair and, from that time on, she understandably refused to sleep in the room.

The next incident was not of a physical nature and involved the first independent witness. A friend of the daughter was staying overnight in the bedroom where the previous activity had occurred; the mother had gone out for the evening and was not expected back till the early hours of the morning. The visiting friend knew nothing of the problems the family had experienced and went to bed completely oblivious to the previous activity in the room she was now sleeping in. Over breakfast the visitor enquired as to who the old lady was that had visited her and stooped over the bed during the night? Fearful that the family secret might get out, the daughter suggested that she must have dreamed it, though later she realised that it could have been her mother checking on their guest. However, later that day her mother denied that she had been anywhere near the room, going straight to bed when returning from her night out.

Some weeks later the daughter saw the old lady for herself standing at the foot of her bed. She reported that she felt quite calm as the apparition seemed to smile at her before turning and disappearing through the closed door, which was certainly not as terrifying an experience as her earlier ones. The family now began to think that they must have two different spirit entities in their house, one intent on causing havoc and the other a pleasant and calming influence. To resolve the situation they decided to use a Ouija board to try and find out some further details about who or what was haunting them. They co-opted some close friends to help them, disguising the true objective of the session by saying it was just for fun. Some weeks later there were five of them seated in a darkened front room with only two candles for illumination, and they were soon to regret their choice of communication method with their visitors.

Almost immediately the board began to spell out some words that put apprehension into the minds of those around the table, and at the same time whoever or whatever was communicating with them refused to answer questions on identity. The movements of the glass became both more erratic and forceful until finally it flew off the board. The group were reluctant to resume their investigation at this point; however, they decided to be brave and to carry on, and soon noticed that the pace and answers were changing. The board told them that they were communicating with a lady called Grace and they soon determined that she was the wife of the first tenant of that house. She told them that she had lived there with her husband, and then when he had died she had lived with her daughter's family until she passed into the spirit world. Her task now was to act as guardian on the other side in order to protect vulnerable occupants from a particularly nasty discarnate entity. They were asked to call on her if they had any more poltergeist activity and she would take action to halt it permanently. To date the poltergeist activity has ceased completely, although they claim to still see Grace from time to time.

Some may believe this tale, whilst others will go with the scientific answer that it was psychokinesis brought on by the girl's emotional state, though the thought of a guardian spirit watching over the house is an intriguing proposition.

However, we do know that the records of the 1901 census show that a Grace and her husband were indeed living at the address at that time, whilst other birth and death certificates also confirm the information given from beyond the grave. Which explanation do you believe?

Private Residence, Stow Hill, Newport Town

Stow Hill is in the oldest part of Newport, and it was here in the 1830s that the Newport workhouse was erected. Over the next forty years the workhouse site on the south side of Stow Hill was gradually enlarged and equipped with an infirmary and a hospital, before being largely demolished and rebuilt at the turn of the twentieth century. In addition to the workhouse itself (where we now find St Woolos Hospital), Stow Hill also provided shelter for vagrants and a children's home.

Moving forward to the present day, it is in this area of Newport that we find the house at the centre of this fascinating little story. If you walk up Stow Hill from the centre of town, the house is on the right-hand side in the close vicinity of the cathedral. The house has a rather symmetrical style, very common in the Georgian period, and sits in a raised position looking back through railings towards the busy road below. Nearby there are the beautiful regency style houses of Victoria Place, built in the 1840s by the same men who designed the docks to give greater access to Stow Hill.

It is thought that a previous owner of the house may have been one Lord Tredegar, who in his time leased the premises out to a series of different tenants. With all of the usual changes to road layouts and house numbering, it is difficult to trace the exact history of the house, although towards the end of the 1800s records suggest that it was in the hands of a family of school teachers. What we do know is that by the turn of the century the house was occupied by the Ponsford family, and it was following their business difficulties that the house reverted to the Newport Corporation. After this, the house served as a children's home for more than fifty years. After lying empty for a few years, the house was finally bought from the council and went back into private ownership. The new owner moved in with his young family and it was in these early days of their time living there that the new occupants, who were no great believers in the paranormal, experienced a series of very strange and mysterious incidents.

By the early 1980s, the owner of this house had a young son who would have been about five years old. His bedroom was located at the front of the house and its window can clearly be seen from the road outside; looking at the house, this particular window was at the top left of the building. One night, the owner of the house heard a child's voice calling from the direction of his son's bedroom. The voice was clearly heard calling out the word 'Daddy' and demanding attention. Obviously assuming that this was his young son calling out, he

Stow Hill, Newport, looking down to the town centre.

made his way to the bedroom. On entering the room, the man discovered that the young boy was sleeping soundly and the calling promptly stopped!

In these early years in the house, this particular owner had this experience five or six times, always hearing the voice from the same room and usually, but not always, when occupied by a child. As the owner entered the room the calling would always stop abruptly.

As the voice of the child became more familiar, it was less upsetting and unnerving, but nonetheless extremely puzzling. As the owner's own child grew up the calling became less and less frequent until finally it stopped altogether. No satisfactory explanation was ever found to rationalise what might have been happening.

After some years passed, the owner met a man who had been a child in the house many years before. They talked of the time when the house was a children's home. Unprompted, the visitor spoke about the 'haunted' room and before he went any further, the owner knew precisely which room it would be. Even in the days when he had been a young child himself, the now middle-aged man confirmed that the room had the very strong reputation of being haunted.

Rumour has it that a lonely boy had killed himself in that room – but we do not know the truth for sure and may never do so. In 2008, after thirty years, the house was sold again and is now in the hands of new owners. By this time it had been a good many years since the sound of the young child had been heard and hopefully the spirit of the lonely child, if that is what it was, is now at rest.

Necropolis, Stow Hill, Newport Town

The slopes of Stow Hill, in what is now the city of Newport, have been lived on since prehistoric times. Its inhabitants have, from the earliest times through to the present day, regarded the area around the top of the hill as a sacred site. It is no surprise therefore to find St Woolos Cathedral placed at the very highest point, where a church has stood since Saxon times. If you take a look at the stones in the walls of this structure you will also find remnants in the shape of ancient standing stones incorporated into the medieval structure. These stones indicate that this was probably an ancient pagan site far before the advent of Christianity. The church probably remained alone on the hill until the eighteenth century when rich merchants and industrialists started to build their houses with good views of the landscape, town, docks and factories in the Usk Valley below. The major suburban settlement on Stow Hill we see today did not come into being till the mid-nineteenth century. We must bear all this in mind when we consider the following accounts.

These following events happened in houses in Clifton Road and St Woolos Road, some of which are now in commercial use. The first occurred in the 1980s soon after a family had moved into the property across the road from the cathedral. It was only after they had put all their furniture in place that they thought to venture into the cellar in order to store what they did not immediately need. Although they expected it to be cold down there as the cellar area was unheated, they did not expect to experience the low temperature they encountered as they reached the bottom of the stairs. After taking a few things down, the husband noticed a foul smell in the place. He saw that the main pipe to the sewer crossed the ceiling and exited through the wall; however, a quick examination showed no breaks or leaks in the pipe.

Old postcard showing trams on Stow Hill, Newport.

The same type of coldness and smell was detected many times over the next months, so they called in a surveyor to examine the property. The survey turned up nothing as the sewage discharge system was found to be intact, and even a gas monitor left in the cellar failed to register either a gas leak or natural methane leaking through the flagstone floor.

Due to these phenomena, they tried not to use the cellar area. However, one day the wife was alone in the house when she heard noises coming from the cellar door. One part of her wanted to investigate but the other told her not to, so she waited for her husband to return with the children. Suspecting that rats might be the cause of all their troubles, he carefully opened the door and descended the stairs. A quick examination showed nothing there, nor were there any traces of rat droppings or that packaging material had been eaten. Even so, he felt sure that some trunks stored there had been moved, and patches on the floor that were clear of dust seemed to indicate this. His wife and children confirmed that they had not been down there for months and even when they had, they had not moved anything. It was some months later while the family were in the lounge watching television that they heard several dull thuds coming from the cellar. Telling the rest of his family to stay put, the husband rushed down to the cellar.

The sight that greeted him was bizarre, as the furniture, trunks and other items had all been moved to the sides of the cellar, leaving a large clear space in the centre. However, he also felt a presence with him in the room, as if something was watching his every move. This was the first time they had even considered that their cellar was haunted. From that point on they locked the cellar door and it remained that way until they moved from the premises some ten years later. When they moved, it was said that one of the removal men refused to go back down into the cellar, but would not tell his colleagues why...

The next story is also about a cellar in a house in nearby Clifton Road. The house had been converted to offices some years before, and the owner did not know what to do with the cellar as it was not suitable for office space and he thought it too damp for storage. It was decided to make it into a small canteen and kitchen for the office staff. The house was duly occupied and every available room was in use, including the kitchen, which was used by all the staff. The staff eventually suggested that their employer could supply sandwiches and hot snacks, as although it was fine going down to the city centre, the steep climb back up was a problem in the time allotted. The management agreed with the request and employed someone part-time to look after the catering. It is from the person they employed in the canteen that we hear the following chilling tale. Initially everything was fine and the facility was proving very popular, but things were soon about to change.

The first indication of what was to come took place when she was alone clearing up after the lunchtime rush. She claimed that a feeling that there was someone else in the room began to come over her. She dismissed it as the product of an overactive imagination, but after it had happened a few times more she started to become a little apprehensive. It was a dismal winter's day when things started to escalate, with the appearance of what she described as a shadowy figure lurking in the corner. She needed the job and was reluctant to either report her experience or resign. However, the decision was going to be made for her as she next witnessed an apparition that she described as the faint outline of a body wrapped in bindings, reminiscent of an Egyptian mummy. Although she never saw the apparition again, a series of shoves, prods and pinches made her a bag of nerves. For the sake of her sanity she reluctantly decided to leave her employment. She has not heard of any further activity in that building and she thinks it may have been something that, for some unknown reason, picked on her and her alone.

On hearing the story, a friend of the lady who was interested in local history volunteered to carry out some research on the area. On looking at some nineteenth-century maps she soon found a possible explanation for the hauntings. It turned out that the whole of the area had, until the turn of the century, been a cemetery complete with a Victorian necropolis. Further research revealed that there was also a mortuary on the site where corpses would have been prepared for internment. Perhaps this apparition was a person who was prepared and embalmed without being dead and was still trying to tell people of the mistake. Although burials in the Victorian cemetery were exhumed and reburied elsewhere before the houses were built, there is evidence that the area was used for burials in ancient times. Could it be that the remains of ancient inhabitants of this area still lie beneath the cellars of these and other houses in the area?

Private Residence, Pontypool

Mark has been living in his house in Pontypool, situated on a quiet cul-de-sac not far from Pontypool Park, since 1979. The house was built in the late nineteenth century and there are actually some pictures of it in some Pontypool history books dating back to the early twentieth century.

It was during the 1980s when strange things started occurring in and around Mark's house. The living room has two windows which look out to the driveway situated at the side of the house, while the driveway itself is closed off with two sturdy metal gates, and at the other end is a tall fence and locked wooden gate. On numerous occasions, Mark and other members of his family have witnessed unusually fast-moving dark figures passing by the windows. Although they have rushed to see who might be trespassing on their driveway, when they look outside there's no sign of anyone or any indication that either the metal gates or the wooden gate have been used. Mark describes the figures as being around 5ft 11in in height, but other than that none of his family have ever been quick enough to see any detail of these mysterious figures. What were they wearing? Are they male or female? No one seems to know.

The figures are seen all year long, during the daytime and even late into the evening in the summer months when the family have left their curtains open. The family dining room also has a window overlooking the same side of the house, yet beyond the wooden gate and onto the back garden as well. Amazingly, these speedy figures have been seen walking past this window too. Various members of the family – both those who are resident and also those visiting – have seen these figures, so Mark is now convinced it's not just his imagination playing tricks on him!

One member of Mark's family has taken a bit more convincing. A disbeliever in ghosts and the paranormal, this particular family member had a very strange experience one day while visiting Mark. While sat in the living room, he was surprised to see what he assumed to be a delivery person walking up the driveway and he assumed they were leaving a parcel around

The shelves and paintbrushes that mysteriously appeared on the floor of Mark's garage.

the side of the house as if not receiving an answer at the front door. However, not only had he not heard anyone try the front door, but it's highly unlikely any delivery person would be brave enough to access the driveway as at that time Mark had a rather large Rottweiler patrolling the area! The family had plenty of signs warning visitors of the dog's presence, specifically around the front gate and driveway area, so no sane delivery person would access this entrance. The confused family member rushed to the back door, expecting to meet the delivery person and the dog barking and growling. However, upon opening the back door, there was not a soul in sight anywhere, the front drive gates were closed and the dog was fast asleep!

One morning at around 7 a.m. in July 2008, Mark had a rather strange experience of a different kind in his house, more specifically in his garage, which is situated at the back of the house at the bottom of the garden. He entered the garage in the usual way, through the electric garage doors, and as he walked through the building towards the back of his mother's car, he was surprised to see two small shelves and two paint brushes laid out on the floor. Not only were they not in that position the previous night, but they were almost 'laid out' in a very specific fashion. Both of the shelves were laid out with the fronts on the floor, one behind the other, and the two paint brushes were opposite each other. Mark is adamant that these shelves could not have simply fallen off the wall because they had been securely attached to the roofing joints and had been there for a considerable period of time without so much as a wobble. Also, the brushes had been on the back of a separate shelving unit mounted on the nearby wall. Nothing else from these wall shelves had been disturbed and even if they had, the chances of the roof joist shelving and brushes from elsewhere in the garage suddenly falling to the ground and landing alongside each other in such a specific fashion is nearing the impossible!

Mark has tried pushing the shelves and brushes from their original positions to the floor, to see if they land in a similar position to that of which he found them, but to no avail.

He was the last person to enter the garage the night before, and he's sure that they were not there as he locked up. No one can access the garage overnight either as the electricity supply to the garage is turned off. So who, or what, caused the falling items, and why were they placed so carefully on the floor? Maybe Mark's last story has an answer.

In August 2008, Mark was in the garage cleaning his car when he turned around to look towards his mother's car after hearing a small noise. Looking through the windows of her car, Mark was amazed to see a small boy smiling back at him! The boy had long, curly brown hair and his left-hand front tooth was missing. Glancing up over the top of the car to get a better look, and to ask him who he was and how he got in, Mark was astounded to find that the little boy had vanished into thin air.

Mark has done some research into the history of his house and has discovered that the side where the driveway now stands had previously been part of the route of a public footpath. Could it be that the spirits of some of the people who used to walk the footpath are still treading the same route all these years later?

Newport Area

Looking at the city of Newport and its surroundings today you would be hard pressed to identify Roman sites, let alone any from the Iron Age or the late Stone Age, but humans have occupied the area since the earliest periods of our history. The evidence can often be found in the names of specific areas that have been passed down over time. Langstone, for example, takes its name from a tall standing stone that was once in the area. Then there are the numerous Iron Age fort sites named Caer, and even what is left of a prehistoric burial chamber, Gwern y Cleppa, next to the M4 across a bridge from the Celtic Springs Business Park. Talking of springs, there are also many springs and wells that have been transposed from sacred sites through Christian holy sites to virtual obscurity today. With the expansion of Newport in the seventeenth and eighteenth centuries, little heed was paid to either ancient megaliths or the network of springs that ran beneath the town. The stones probably ended up in other structures, as in St Woolos Cathedral, and the wells and springs became so contaminated that they were capped or filled in. For example, there is a record of an order in 1901 directing that 'Beans Well' be filled in as it was contaminated with effluvia and rats. Then there is the site of 'Eves Well' that was ordered to be fenced off due to a mixture of folklore and hearsay about it being an entry to beyond the grave. It was named after a particularly troublesome ghost that had haunted a local village and, after being chased across the countryside, was allegedly last seen disappearing down the well.

No wonder then that the souls of people down the ages are disturbed with what modern man is doing to places they held sacred. Perhaps the long-dead show their displeasure through paranormal activity? Our first event concerns a man who lodged on Chepstow Road, to the east of the city. He claimed to have always had an open mind about ghosts and haunting, but had had no real experience of such activity until that day. The lodger had been out that evening and after returning sat up watching late night television and eventually turned in some time after midnight. He did not sleep at all well, and for some unknown reason started to become apprehensive, getting more and more nervous as

Old postcard of Commercial Street, Newport town centre, c. 1917.

the night progressed. The room was getting progressively colder so he got up to check the radiator. However, it proved to be piping hot. Pulling the duvet around him he still appeared to be getting colder and started to physically shiver.

He claimed that he was now very scared indeed, thinking either that he was ill or some unseen supernatural force was responsible for the situation. The latter seemed more probable as a feeling of anguish and hatred seemed to envelop him. He thought this menacing energy was coming from the opposite corner of the room and although there was nothing to see, there was plenty to sense. The temperature in the room still appeared to be dropping, and with it the sense of loathing and malevolence grew more intense. Although he had no idea how, he knew that whatever it was wanted him and his kind out of there. He managed to survive the night and soon things were back to normal. Several weeks later the landlady decided to sell the house and it was with some relief that he had to find new lodgings. Some years later he met a local medium and she informed him that an ancient spirit had possessed the house where he had lived since it had been built. She also claimed that old maps showed an ancient stone row in roughly that location and this was the probable cause of the activity.

Not far from that location is the large housing estate of Ringland, where many people have observed paranormal activity. A woman reported feeling a cold, icy blast go past her whilst she was on her way home one night. Another sensed a menacing presence following her after she alighted from the bus, which followed her till she reached her front door. Both witnesses say that there was nothing to see, only this overpowering feeling and an icy coldness. In the centre of the estate is an open area with probably the last remaining trees of Flat Wood, which originally covered this site. Here several people have reported seeing shadowy shapes moving around the trees. It has been speculated that this was, in fact, an ancient sacred site and that the architects and planners had been subliminally guided to create a similar circle or ring in the centre of this housing complex.

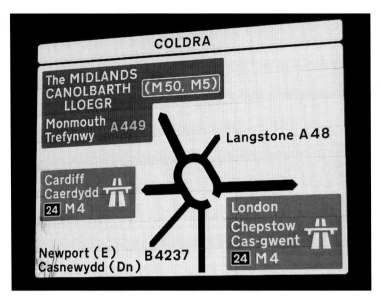

The Coldra interchange, Newport.

Perhaps the most interesting incident to happen in this area took place as a man was going home from Llanwern Steelworks in the early hours of the morning. The man's father was on his deathbed and had taken a turn for the worse. He was given permission to leave his shift and go to the Royal Gwent Hospital to be with his mother as his father ebbed away. He decided that the quickest way would be to use the motorway and so he headed for the Coldra interchange. As he approached the roundabout a figure stepped out into the road in front of him. From what he remembered, the man was dressed in some sort of full-length white robe, held a staff in one hand and had a bearded face that looked straight at him. Seconds later he had passed straight through what turned out to be an apparition and the road both behind and in front of him was clear. Unfortunately, he did not make it to the hospital in time to see his father before he passed away, but discovered his life ended at around the same time he had his strange and paranormal experience These days he still wonders whether the apparition was a messenger sent to tell him that his father had passed on, or the spirit of an ancient who once roamed this area. In Wales there is a long folk tradition of so-called 'Wake Ghosts'.

It is important to remember the words of the great Native American Chief Seattle:

When the last of ancients have left the earth and their memory among modern men has become myth and folklore, our lands will swarm with the spirits of our ancestors. Even when your children's children shall think themselves alone in the field, the store, the shop, upon the road or street, or in the silence of the woods, they will not be alone. In all the earth there is no place dedicated to solitude. At night, when the streets of your cities, towns and villages are silent and you think them deserted, actually they will teem with the returning hosts that once filled and still love this beautiful world. Modern mankind will never be alone. Let him be just and think kindly of ancient peoples, for the dead are not powerless.

Private Residence, Cwmbran

Once you have crossed the A4042 from Cwmbran, you are plunged into a world of isolated farms and houses fed by a sparse system of lanes, some of which soon deteriorate into tracks that eventually peter out into woods or fields. The couple that related this tale had been renting an ancient farmhouse in just such a location. In fact, inclement weather like heavy rain or snow effectively isolated them from the nearest metalled road, which was some three miles away. Although they had mains electricity this was often interrupted and they had to rely on mobile phones for their contact with the outside world on a daily basis. To the happy couple, however, it was a wonderful opportunity to live in a period farmhouse in the middle of some beautiful surroundings, and yet still commute to Newport every day to work in the city. Often when the weather was not kind, they had to abandon their car at the end of the made-up lane, don their boots and walk the last mile home. It is against this background that our strange tale unfolds.

They had been resident in the farmhouse for only a few months when one night they were awakened by a loud noise over and above the typical sounds of the countryside at this hour. The noise then subsided and the couple returned to sleep. Some nights later they had just gone to bed when, to their surprise, they heard the noise yet again and this time they identified it as a screeching or a scream, and it was coming from the direction of the wood across the valley. They were concerned that something untoward was happening and being conscientious citizens they quickly dressed, grabbed some torches and headed towards the source of the noise. The noise having ceased for the time being, they then also grew concerned for their car that they had been forced to leave that night, as there had been isolated cases of vandalism on some local farms. A blood-curdling scream rang once more across the valley from the woods ahead where their car waited, and they began to grow more apprehensive in their approach. It took them some time to reach their car, as it was a dark night with cloud cover and a hint of rain in the air.

The car was covered with a fine mist of water from the drizzle, but there was no physical evidence that anybody had been near it. They then decided, reluctantly, to turn their attention to the woods and check out several options they did not even want to think about. The first was that some dastardly deed had been, or was still being, committed in the wood, and the second was that the screams were supernatural in their nature. There was no physical evidence of another vehicle, nor had they heard any engines, so they decided that the first option was somewhat doubtful. The couple agreed it was very unlikely that someone would be able to lure their victim this far off from the beaten track on foot. As they came to a bend in the track they both saw an eerie light in the dense trees ahead, which was quickly extinguished as they approached. The pair did not know what to think now and decided to call it a night and examine the area in the cold light of day.

On the way to work they carried out a quick examination of the woods' edge, but it revealed nothing of interest. There was no evidence of human intervention as the undergrowth appeared undisturbed and only the runs made by small animals were visible to them. On their way up to the main road they were halted by a tractor and trailer parked in the lane. A man who they did not recognise suddenly arrived out of breath and apologised for holding them up. He introduced himself as the son of the farmer and said it was a long time since he had worked on the farm and he had not got back into the routine of shutting the gates to prevent cattle straying. It transpired that his father was very ill and the farm worker who usually helped him had to go to market that day so he was helping out. They decided to ask whether he was staying at the farm or not as a prelude to asking some questions about the screams.

Unfortunately he had only arrived that morning and had to go back to his building business once the hired help had arrived back. The husband decided to ask the question anyway as he was probably brought up on the farm. The answer, when it came, was inconclusive as he said that there were many strange noises in the countryside and that the cries of a rabbit being killed by a fox were often confused with human screaming. Then there was the screech of an owl that also sounded very much like the cry described. They thanked the farmer's son and followed him to the main road where they went on their way, reassured that there was probably nothing concerning about their experiences.

The next night, however, brought with it more screaming from the woods and the couple decided to investigate in order to get some sort of answer to the questions running around their minds. Once again the pair tramped down to the woods, determined to lay the mystery of the phantom screamer to rest for good. As they approached the stream that followed the valley floor, they both saw a dark anomalous shape that appeared to be following the stream. The wood seemed devoid of any life at all, let alone rabbits or owls, with the sound of the running water in the stream the only noise in the still night air. Looking to the neighbouring farmhouse on the hillside some three miles in the distance, they saw what appeared to be lights traversing towards it. Suspecting that the owners were having some trouble with the animals, resulting in the need to go into the fields at night with torches, they thought nothing more of it. With nothing else they could do, they headed back to the warmth of their home, and from that night on they had no more experiences during their time in this rented accommodation. However, some months later they learnt of an interesting dimension to their experiences. They once again met the farmer's son on the lane and on asking how his father was, he replied that he had died the very night they had last spoken.

The Gwrach y Rhibyn, according to Welsh folklore, is a particularly obnoxious variety of apparition believed to foretell death. Reputedly, this spectre of an old hag is rarely seen by visitors or newcomers, only revealing herself to those families whose ancestors have lived for generations in the same place. Those that have seen her liken her countenance to the archetypal witch, having long black hair, a swarthy countenance and black eyes which are said to be sunken and emit a piercing stare. Her back is said to be crooked, and her body very thin and covered by black robes.

However, her most salient feature is the high-pitched wailing or screams often heard by even those that do not see her. She is also long associated with 'Corpse Lights', which are said to manifest prior to a death in the area. It is hard to believe that such a creature had been heard and such lights seen in these recent times not far from Cwmbran, but having heard the screams and seen unusual lights on the very night this farmer passed away, it does make the couple wonder whether they had their very own encounter with a character long spoken of in Welsh folklore.

five

Spectres of the Great Outdoors

From hooded monks and phantom stagecoaches to arms reaching from beyond the grave, this chapter contains some of the most interesting and unusual tales of the paranormal we have come across, and the one thing they have in common is that they all took place outdoors. Although most ghost stories we hear involve a building, there have long been people reporting things when they are out and about; spooky roads and woods have often featured in books. Perhaps, however, far more people have seen something paranormal and not realised that they have done so due to the more open and unknown surroundings. We would suggest that in the future, when you drive down a dark and quiet road or wander through some woodland at dusk, that you keep your senses open and who knows, maybe you will encounter an outdoor spectre...

Bassaleg, West Newport

Keith is originally from Cwmcarn, which lies approximately ten miles north of Bassaleg. An electrician by trade, Keith is now retired, but he has been a resident of Bassaleg for over forty years to date, and lives about a mile and a half from the very heart of the village. It is thought that the comparatively modern housing estate to the north-west of the centre of Bassaleg, where Keith now lives, may be built on lands that once belonged to a priory which was erected there after the Norman Conquest. Certainly this area would appear to lie across the ancient pathways through the woods that have long been associated with the old priory.

At least two apparitions of monks have been seen around this very area. They appear to trudge the old priory paths and lands as they would have done many hundreds of years ago. One of the monks is believed to bring significant comfort at times of trouble and despair. This particular spirit is known to have appeared at times of tragedy and difficulty, and although it would not be appropriate to share the personal details of individuals' situations, several local people believe this to be the case given their own experiences of this joyous spectre. Appearing at such times as these would be very much in keeping with the original mission of the monks, and in their own times they would have performed many works of

Above: *The picturesque river than runs through Bassaleg.*

Right: *A Benedictine monk, scanned from* English Monastic Life *by F.A. Gasquet, published in 1904 by Methuen & Co., London.*

charity, helping to heal the sick or feeding the hungry who were brought to their doors. They may also have provided medicines to those who were in need.

The good monk who has been seen in Bassaleg is reported as being rather tall, something in the region of 6ft in height. While seen from a distance by some, Keith has seen him particularly close up as he travels the ancient pathways. He has even seen beneath the cowl of the hooded figure, as this particular monk is usually seen with his hood lowered and resting around his shoulders. He describes the monk as being fairly young, with a slight ginger colouring and a fresh and clear complexion. He is always alone, sometimes caught in the headlamps of a car, but at other times much, much closer. The one thing that all of the descriptions do have in common is that he appears to be plainly dressed in a black habit.

It is an established historical fact that there was a Benedictine priory in Bassaleg. The colour of the habits varied according to their order. Black became the prevailing colour of the Benedictine monks' clothes and so the term 'Black Monks' will usually be in reference to a monk from the Benedictine order. The Cistercians, for example, who had even stricter rules than the Benedictines, used un-dyed wool for their monks' habits in an effort to show their poverty. Their habits would be greyish-white or brown and they would often be known as 'White Monks'.

For the Benedictine monk there was always a very strong separation between the monastic life and that of the outside world. The monastery would form an independent, self-supporting settlement and the monks would have no need to go outside for anything on a day-to-day basis. They could be surprisingly large establishments, covering many acres and starting to take on the appearance of a fortified town. The Benedictine monks lived under strict discipline. In addition to all the vows that they were instructed to take, they were also not allowed to go beyond the monastery walls without the consent of the abbot himself. This suggests that the monk seen in Bassaleg is more than likely to be walking in an area that would at one time have been priory land within the confines of the monastery walls. Old maps confirm that the areas where the monk has been seen fit with this theory.

It seems that our good monk may also have company, as another monk-like figure has also been seen around the area, but with his hood raised he cuts a somewhat more frightening figure to those who encounter him. However, in truth there is nothing to suggest that he is anything other than benign. On one occasion in the recent past, Keith was attending a golden wedding celebration at a venue in Caerphilly. Here he met a young man who earned his living as a driver and they went on to converse for some time. When the driver heard which village Keith came from, he related a story of when he last drove through Bassaleg himself. He explained that he was driving over the river near to St Basil's Church, a church thought to be dedicated to St Gwladys, hermit and wife of St Gwynllyw, when he caught a cowled figure in the headlamps of his van. He was absolutely convinced of the reality of what he had seen, and he went on to say that as he first saw the figure from the front, he also then saw it again, reflected back in his mirrors. The hooded figure was clearly skeletal in appearance, not the same warm and friendly looking figure that Keith and so many others had experienced!

The history of the priory in Bassaleg was to be comparatively brief, as although it was founded about 1,000 years ago, within 100 years it was closed. Virtually every trace of the priory is now gone, but it does appear that the same cannot be said about the monks of Bassaleg.

Redwick, South-East Newport

The village of Redwick is set on the Gwent levels just a few miles to the south-east of Newport. Redwick is well known for the Church of St Thomas, which is a large and impressive church for such a small village. In addition to its size, it is remarkable for its many other unusual features. The earliest parts of the building date from the fourteenth century, although there are also many more recent restorations. The church retains the remnants of a medieval rood screen and loft, and a beautiful thirteenth-century font, while the medieval stone carvings include an unusual one of a Green Man which is well worth seeing. In addition to all this, the Redwick Church bells, which were cast in Bristol, are among the oldest in the country that remain in regular use.

There is one quite well-known legend of a ghost that attaches itself to this part of Redwick, which centres on a most interesting character called Tom, the Squire of Redwick. The story states that he was found dead in a ditch after a drunken night of carousing in the local public houses. It was not long before his ghost, with an unquenchable thirst,

Left: *Redwick churchyard.*

Below: *The marker in Redwick Church that represents the height of the 'great flood'.*

started to steal cider from the local brewers and was seen staggering around the village in a state of inebriation. It appeared to those who witnessed this phenomenon that Tom had no desire to end his fun-loving and drunken ways just because he was no longer a living being! However, it is said that this apparition has long-since been exorcised and he seems not to have been seen around Redwick for some considerable time. Maybe he drank one too many paranormal pints?

On a far more serious note than the drunken squire, the village is also well known for its connection with the great flood of January 1607. This was the worst inundation of the land by storm floods that this area – which was largely reclaimed from the sea – has ever experienced. Originally the 1607 flood was considered to be a mighty storm, but it is something that many now consider to have been a tsunami. There are scientific reasons for believing that the event was more than just a severe flood, while some historical accounts also indicate that the weather was fine at the time and that the speed of the wave appears to have been far greater than that of a normal storm flood. The monstrous waves may have been caused by a landslide or earthquake under the sea between Ireland and Cornwall. Whatever the cause, the effect was devastating as the torrent of water became constricted by the Bristol Channel and then the narrower Severn Estuary. The wave was increasing in size all the time and its height was thought to be some 25ft by the time it hit this part of the Monmouthshire coast. In all, the great flood affected nearly 600km of coastline, leaving the population devastated with at least 2,000 fatalities according to one contemporary source.

The event has not been forgotten in South Wales and it is recorded on plaques in a number of the churches. In addition to the plaques, Redwick Church also has a mark on the wall indicating the high level of the inundation.

The interesting history of Redwick has always attracted visitors, and nearly 400 years after the flood, in the middle of the 1980s, a lady by the name of Ellen was planning to make a visit to St Thomas's Church. She was to be accompanied by a friend who knew the area well; he was a local man from Caldicot and had visited the church many times. Her friend was very keen to show Ellen the famous tidemark preserved on the wall, and also hoped that they could spend some time having a look at the ancient gravestones with their unusual epitaphs, several of which were said to be related to the great tidal wave. On the evening in question the light was starting to fade slightly as they approached the church, but they were still able to see clearly enough as they made their way up the path to this historic building. Going through the gate at the front, they approached the church through the graveyard and walked towards the porch on the right-hand side. Many of the tombs which they passed near to the church entrance were comparatively modern and these ones would not have dated back to the time of the great flood, although the plots themselves would surely have been re-used over the long history of St Thomas's.

Ellen's companion was a well-built man who was used to an outdoor life working around the Severn Estuary, but he stopped in his tracks as they approached the big church door. He was suddenly freezing cold, as cold as he had ever been in his life, and he stated that he could go no further. Ellen was puzzled, but seeing how frozen her companion had become, did not press the matter any further as he was clearly in some distress. Back at the car she asked him what had happened and he explained with some difficulty just what he had seen and felt. He said that as they approached the door, he could see that one of the graves had the appearance of being open and, even stranger than this, that there were arms reaching out from within the grave. It was a truly traumatic sight which had scared him half to death.

On many other occasions the two of them went out together to sites around the Severn Estuary, and never again did he have any further sightings of this nature. Ellen knew him for a further twenty years and he remained as down to earth and knowledgeable about the area as before and absolutely not the sort to be given to dramatic flights of fancy. However the experience clearly had a profound effect on him, and he never mentioned again what he saw on that strange day outside St Thomas's Church.

Who could have been on the other end of those arms reaching out from the grave? Could there be a connection to the famous flood of 1607? We may never know the truth behind this unusual experience, but it would be very interesting to know if anyone else has had a similar thing happen to them!

Pontypool Park, Pontypool

Pontypool Park covers sixty-four hectares of land and is now home to Pontypool Rugby Football Club, who have their pitch there. There is also a leisure centre, dry ski slope and many areas for a lovely, relaxing, scenic walk.

A postcard of the park gates at Pontypool Park, c. 1930.

Back in 1703 the park was first laid out as a private estate for the Hanbury family, who had their wonderful stately home built there. In 1829 they built the 'Shell Grotto' on one of the hills in the park and used this as a summer house. This interesting little creation was covered on the inner walls with animal bones and shells. From the Grotto you can see Pontypool, Abergavenny and, on a very sunny day, even as far as Newport. Currently Hanbury House is the home of St Albans Roman Catholic School and the stable area is now Pontypool Museum.

In 1765, John Hanbury had the 'Folly Tower' built on another part of their land. It is said to be built on the spot where a Roman watchtower had originally been erected. Later, in 1831, it was renovated by Capel Hanbury Leigh, but in the Second World War it was knocked down. Locals unfortunately thought it could be used as an easy landmark for the German Luftwaffe, and as a clear indication of the proximity of the nearby Royal Ordinance Factory at Glascoed which was a suspected bombing target. It was not until 1992 that work started on rebuilding the tower. Around 175 tonnes of dressed stone were donated by the recently demolished local Cwmffrwdoer Primary School and it was then officially reopened on 22 July 1994 by the Prince of Wales.

A young local man, Mark, has had two very strange experiences in and around this much-loved parkland, the first of which occurred in the autumn of 1984.

It was a particularly clear day, the weather having recently turned cooler. Mark and his sister had been watching Pontypool play a rugby match with their dad and they were about to start making their way home. Mark recalls that the time was around 8.30 p.m. as they were heading back across the park. Although the sun had already set and the park itself was relatively dark, the nearby streetlights were lighting the walkways and paths through the park sufficiently enough that they could see clearly and felt perfectly safe.

The river running through Pontypool Park.

They walked through the park heading towards St Albans School and near the school walls they could see the children's play area. Although a normal enough play area with slides and swings, there was also a large wooden 'fort' structure built within – an ideal place for children to run around, climb and hide in. As the three of them walked by, Mark and his sister were amazed to see someone in the fort. Not a child, but a woman. On closer inspection they noticed that the woman was dressed in very strange clothes; a long, Victorian-style grey dress that flowed down to her feet, a wide hat, and she was carrying a large umbrella, currently closed and being used by the mysterious woman as a walking stick. Mark has made it very clear that this mysterious woman was not an old lady, but probably someone who was in her late thirties or early forties.

Mark and his sister stopped dead, staring at her. What was a strangely dressed woman doing in the playground at this time of night? She didn't acknowledge the presence of the two siblings and carried on walking as if they weren't there.

Suddenly, to their amazement, the lady vanished into thin air! Mark and his sister looked at each other in shock. Had they truly just seen a woman vanish in front of their eyes? Upon looking at his sister, Mark knew for sure that she had just seen exactly what he had. Mark quietly asked his sister, who seemed to have turned a strange pale colour, whether she too had just seen an unusually dressed lady vanish into thin air. Upon confirming that she had just witnessed the same phenomena, they both ran towards where the area the lady had vanished.

A postcard of the Grotto in Pontypool Park, c. 1920.

From the darkness behind them, they could both hear the sound of their names being called. Both siblings stopped dead, looked at each other, their hearts beating double time. Slowly they turned towards the sound.

Out of the darkness appeared their father. He was jogging towards them, calling after them, wondering what had grabbed their attention so much that they had run off the path. Breathing a sigh of relief, Mark and his sister described what they had seen – the woman, her strange clothes and her vanishing act, much to the surprise of their father. Mark, being an open-minded young man, likes to think that maybe this was a past member of the Hanbury family taking a walk around the grounds.

Mark's second experience in the park was in the summer of 2006, and centred around the Grotto. It was a lovely warm summer's afternoon and Mark was walking his dog in the park. The dog was off the lead and was enjoying his freedom, running around and having a good sniff about when the two of them began to walk up the steep hill that led up to the Grotto.

They made it about halfway up the hill when Mark stopped to wait for his dog, who had taken great interest in sniffing a particularly large tree on the way. Mark looked back up the hill to see if there was anyone heading down the hill, just in case he needed to put his pet back on his lead – being a large dog, he could seem quite intimidating to some. Mark noticed a man leaning against a tree. Before he called out to his dog to re-attach the lead, Mark noticed there was something odd about the way the man was dressed and he realised that he wasn't exactly dressed in a modern style. The man was wearing a brown suit which consisted of knee-length trousers, knee-length white socks and a brown flat cap. He was smoking a pipe and looking down the hill at Mark.

Mark's dog then walked by and he glanced down to see what his beloved pet was up to and to put him back on his lead. Upon looking back up the hill, expecting to see the strange man dressed in brown still standing there, Mark was stunned to see that he had completely vanished. Mark made the decision to head further up the hill to try to find out where he had disappeared to.

As they made their way up, two people appeared at the top of the hill and started making their way down towards Mark. He stopped the pair and asked them if they had seen a man dressed in old-fashioned clothes, thinking that there may be some sort of historical event at the Grotto summer house. But all Mark got in response was a very definite, but confused sounding, 'No' accompanied by some very strange looks. Upon reaching the Grotto, Mark found it empty and there was no sign of the man.

Who was this strange man leaning against the tree, and was he watching Mark? If so, why? Did he have some kind of link to this mysterious Grotto?

Ancre Hill, Rockfield

There are many tales of phantom stagecoaches which are supposed to clatter their way at speed across certain parts of the United Kingdom. Many of these stories are little more than legends and yet, just occasionally, there is something slightly more compelling about these stories.

Wales has several tales of phantom stagecoaches, but there is one in particular that seems worthy of further investigation. In January 1965, the *Monmouthshire Beacon* published two

A view of Ancre Hill, Rockfield.

tales of phantom stagecoaches seen on the roads of Monmouthshire. One of these was a tale of a coach and four wild-eyed horses travelling on the Monmouth to Abergavenny road. The story claims that in the village of Rockfield the coach rounds a sharp corner and crashes.

That may well have been the end of it, a story that could be put down to little more than a local legend, but in this case it seems to be one that will not go away. Back at the beginning of the twentieth century, sightings of the coach were comparatively common. Then, in the early months of 1966, the *Beacon* revisited the subject, chronicling another four sightings of coaches in the vicinity. One of these sightings was, once again, the Rockfield coach. The opportunity was also taken to repeat the original tale, this time fleshing out the details and pinning down the original location to Ancre Hill in Rockfield. The author of the Rockfield reports had no knowledge at that time of any historical report of an accident on the road. The stories of the coach would be far more convincing if real evidence of a crash, in the Victorian era and on this stretch of road, could be found.

Rockfield is situated five miles to the north-west of Monmouth. Ancre Hill is a steep road, only half a mile in length, leading off the B4233. Driving past the western end of the road, it is easy to miss the inconspicuous and narrow entrance; the largest nearby landmark is the vineyard which is easily spotted because of the neatly laid-out rows of vines.

Some of the oldest sightings talk of how the phantom coach runs into a wall, then crashes through it and into a field by a small stream. The coach, by this time in ruins, finally comes to rest before disappearing. Looking at nineteenth-century maps of the area it is hard to pinpoint the site. The road does run by the side of a river in places and there is a bridge marked. Today, however, the bridge has gone and there are not really any likely candidates for the brick wall. The road is narrow and in quite poor condition, and seems to have little of the geographical features mentioned in the story to help pinpoint the exact location of the crash. When a few of the current residents of Ancre Hill were asked if they had any recent sightings of the coach, they had nothing to report.

Neil and Ruth, who have been researching the tale, say:

Really we needed to retrace our way back through contemporary accounts of the time. The date of 1850 appears in some accounts, but we were far from convinced about the reliability of that date. The assertion that it is only seen on dark and stormy nights does not necessarily mean that this was the prevailing weather conditions on the night of the original accident, if indeed there had ever been an accident. We really had comparatively little to go on. We thought that surely the local newspaper of the time would carry a story such as this.

However, in the reference libraries of Monmouthshire the collections of local newspapers are not complete and there are large gaps spanning several years. The Monmouth local paper itself could not help, having lost many of their back issues in a fire in 1963. However they did publish Neil and Ruth's letter as they looked for further information on the crash.

The best source of newspapers from that period is at the records office in Monmouth Museum and, with the museum's help, Neil and Ruth spent some hours reading the Victorian papers trying to get to the bottom of the mystery. Even here the copies of the

Ancre Hill, Rockfield.

newspaper were not complete. In 1850, for example, one third of the weekly papers are not to be found in the collection. To date they have found no reference to the crash on Ancre Hill, yet the details could be in one of the 'lost' issues or even in a year falling outside the period they have examined. For the moment they have drawn a blank as far as historical corroboration of the facts are concerned.

Was there ever a phantom coach or was the apparition merely the swirling rain, caught in the headlamps of a car as it bumped over the rough road? Perhaps the wind in the trees could sound a little like the movement of wheels, while the pounding of the rain on the road could remind a listener of the beat of hooves thundering through the night.

Even if there has never been a coach crash on Ancre Hill, there is certainly something slightly unusual and highly atmospheric about the location. Ruth and Neil stated:

> When we last visited Rockfield it was a bright winter's day, but even then it was not hard to imagine how the road might have been 150 years ago on a wild night with horse-drawn coaches making their way down the lane.

The search for the phantom coach goes on; please contact the authors if you may be able to add to this local tale...

The mysterious Harold's Stones at Trellech.

Trellech, South of Monmouth

Trellech sits as part of an ancient landscape stretching back to prehistoric times, and it also contains the physical and unseen imprints of a slice of Welsh history. The Norman invasion, Owain Glyndwr and the Black Death must have all had a negative effect on what was once the second-largest town in the Principality. It is hard to believe that this pretty and quaint rural village between Chepstow and Monmouth was once the site of extensive industry and a large population. You would be hard pressed today to find any evidence of this other than lumps and bumps in the surrounding fields. However, evidence of much earlier occupation is still clearly visible. From the ancient standing stones to a Norman motte and medieval fishponds, we see pointers to Trellech being occupied for a very long time. Let us return to those three megaliths on the edge of the village, from where it gets its Welsh name. They are also known as 'Harold's Stones', named after the English king who is said to have fought a decisive battle on this site although, strangely, who the enemy was is unclear.

This brings us nicely to the rich legends and folk tales that surround this beautiful Gwent village. Folklore tells that Jack O'Kent, who was a folk hero in the borderland of Herefordshire and Monmouthshire, was a wizard with supernatural powers, a trickster who got the better of the Devil himself on more than one occasion, and actually threw the stones there from a dozen miles away in a competition with the Devil.

Inside the church there now sits a seventeenth-century sundial on which is believed to be the earliest written description of the stones. An image of the stones is carved on the base of the sundial and the numbers 7, 10 and 14 are written upon them, possibly indicating the height of the stones when the sundial was first constructed. There is also a stone slab on supports in the churchyard, which local legend says is a Christianised Druidic altar. The village itself also has a holy well, called the 'Virtuous Well' or 'St Anne's Well',

The signs at either end of the village, interestingly with different spellings!

which is said to cure a range of ailments by just soaking a cloth in the water and placing it on the affected part of the body. Archaeologists have also found flint tools in the immediate vicinity, which suggests that this spring has been in use for a very long time indeed.

It is against this historic background of facts, myths and legends that we need to look at some recent mysterious happenings in and around the village. Let us first examine an incident that happened at Harold's Stones a few years ago to a pair of well-known dowsers. They had been surveying the megaliths regularly for many months, but on this particular day they could not keep up with the rapidly changing energy patterns. Suddenly, without warning, an invisible force knocked them both to the ground. Conglomerate rock, or 'pudding stone' as it is sometimes called, contains quartz inclusions distributed throughout. Were these stones therefore acting like a giant capacitor and storing up earth energy, which they then randomly discharged, causing this dramatic effect? The other possibility for the more open minded amongst us is that there was some kind of guardian spirit of the stones that objected to their continual visits and, by some force which we do not fully understand, showed their displeasure in this manner.

Even today some people in the village believe that there is a curse on the Virtuous Well, perhaps with good cause. Recently a man and his wife visited the well, and unfortunately an argument followed as the wife wanted to sit and meditate whilst the husband, being a sceptic, wanted to drive away. On his way back to the car, in something of a sulk, he firstly claimed he was pushed from behind and fell, causing a gash on his forehead that needed stitches at the nearest casualty department. He subsequently claimed that he tripped over a branch put across the path; however, his wife insisted that the path was clear when she rushed to his assistance.

The next incident concerned a visitor to the well who tried to take a frog home in a jam jar. Realising that the amphibian would need air they cut some holes in the lid with a penknife. The next minute they claimed their hand was forced to stab the knife through their other hand! The result was that the frog was released and the unfortunate person was again destined to end up visiting the local hospital.

There are also many tales of incidents, not as dramatic as these two, such as local downpours that prevented people leaving their cars to visit the well. Is there also a guardian of the well that checks people visiting and punishes those they see as committing an offence? Although all small and somewhat vague stories, the sheer number of them connected to this well and the surrounding area would indicate that it deserves further investigation.

Another experience in this fascinating little village concerns a man who had just dropped his wife off at the doctor's surgery in the village at a time when the public car park outside was full. He drove around the corner and pulled into a small lay-by created by the entrance gate to a field and parked. A car soon pulled up on the road in front of him and the driver was at his window. He asked our witness not to park there and became somewhat aggressive when our man told him it was none of his business. It would have come to blows, but for the intervention of this objectionable man's wife. The protagonist's countenance seemed to change immediately when he heard his wife's voice and he appeared both dazed and confused. It soon transpired that he had little recollection of his outburst, only an overwhelming need to stop the man parking there at any cost. Shortly after, a resident of the village who observed the fracas added an interesting dimension to the puzzle. He stated that apparently many years ago a car which had parked in that very spot had been hit by a large lorry, instantly killing the unfortunate occupant. Had the spirit of this victim possessed this passing motorist in order to warn another of the dangers of parking at that spot?

The most intriguing incident in Trellech in recent years received much publicity when it happened during the Millennium year. An eleven-year-old boy was allegedly attacked in a field next to the primary school in the village by a wild animal. He needed medical treatment after he was left with what appeared to be claw marks across his face. The media claimed that experts thought from the boy's description that a 5ft juvenile black leopard might have been the involved. This was headline news in both local and national media in August 2000. When the initial media hype had died down, a group of experts, including two professional big-cat hunters, carried out a fingertip search of the scene and a thorough search of the surrounding locality without finding any evidence or spoors of big cats. Some have cited the boy's injuries as positive proof of big cats loose in the Welsh countryside. However, some working in the paranormal field claim that discarnate beings are also quite capable of inflicting such injuries.

The B4246 from Blaenavon to Abergavenny

The B4246 is the road leading from Blaenavon to Abergavenny, and part of the road is known locally as the 'Fiddlers Elbow'. It is a very tight left-hand bend where the road is very steep and has a gravel escape lane if your brakes fail going down the hill. Unusually, this area is rumoured to be haunted.

The B4246 at Blaenavon.

It is a very scenic road, with moorland on both sides of it, and is part of the Brecon Beacons National Park. There are two quite big car parks at the top; one overlooks a large pond and the other overlooks Abergavenny and the surrounding area. In one of these car parks is the grave of a famous showjumping horse called Foxhunter, who was once owned by Colonel Harry Llewellyn. There is, as you would imagine, a lot of animal life on the moors including red grouse and the local farmers' sheep.

Mark's experience happened in October 2002 at around 9 p.m. He was driving home from Abergavenny and decided not to take his normal route home, which is through the Abergavenny lanes leading to Pontypool, and instead he decided to drive along the Fiddlers Elbow road.

It was a clear, dry evening and the stars were out. Mark turned left to go up the road from Abergavenny and made his way up the steep road, slowing down for the tight left-hand bend, and then he continued along the road where there is a straight section. Ahead of him he could see a small red light, like the ones cyclists use on the back of their bikes, which was moving slowly up the road ahead, weaving slightly as cyclists do when they ride up steep hills. As it reached the next bend in the road, it disappeared out of sight. Mark carried on up the hill and soon got around the bend to where the road straightened up again. Expecting to have caught up with the cyclist and preparing to pull over to the right-hand side of the road to overtake them, he was surprised to find there was no one there! He slowed down in case the cyclist had fallen off somewhere but could see no sign of anyone.

Both sides of the road have a high barbed-wire fence as one side drops down into a very deep quarry and the other side leads to a wooded area, so it wouldn't have been easy for anyone to have taken a detour from the road. Mark looked carefully for the cyclist and the bike, driving slowly in first gear, but was unable to find any trace of anyone.

Mark continued further up the road but saw no one at all; he had not even seen another car going in either direction since witnessing the red light.

He drove up to the first car park by the pond and turned around to go back down the hill and retraced his tracks to see whether he could find anything similar to what he had seen, but still nothing was apparent. Was it perhaps the ghost of a lonely cyclist? Who knows, but Mark has driven on that road many times since then and has never seen the red light again... yet!

Woodland, Caerleon

So I went on and on until I came to the secret wood which must not be described, and I crept into it by the way I had found.

These lines come from the book *The White People* by Arthur Machen, and are believed by some to refer to the very woods near to his birthplace at Caerleon. Arthur was born in Caerleon, on the River Usk, in 1863 and was actually christened Arthur Llewellyn Jones, although he took his mother's maiden name later in life. His father was an Anglican priest, vicar of the tiny church of Llandewi, near Caerleon, and as a boy he was raised at the rectory there. He spent much of his early youth roaming around the area and soaking up the wonderful and fascinating history, mysteries and folklore that surrounded him. In this period he would also have seen many archaeologists digging up the artefacts left during the occupation of Caerleon by the Roman armies. It is no wonder that in later life he became one of the leading authors of his time in the field of mystery, the arcane and horror. The folk tales and legends about the then extensive ancient wood of St Julian's at Christchurch must have proved an invaluable source for his later books.

Today the wood is a beautiful oasis of trees bordering the quaint village of Christchurch, the M4 motorway, the Usk and the outer suburbs of Newport itself. A waymarked public footpath and several tracks cross the wood, offering easy access to keen hikers and those merely walking their dogs. It is from these people that we hear the various stories that will now unfold. You may expect to hear of ghosts associated with marching Roman and Civil War soldiers in view of its position adjacent to a town that saw much activity in both periods of our history. You will, however, be surprised to hear of elementals, fairies and menacing apparitions at this strange location.

The first of these accounts concerns a lady out walking her dog at dusk on an early autumn evening in the early twenty-first century. She had parked her car by Holy Trinity Church and walked happily down the track into the woods, and it was there that she let her faithful dog off the lead. As usual she threw a stick and the dog retrieved it, and this game continued until they came to one part of the wood where her canine friend became excited and started barking at something in the undergrowth. Thinking it was a rabbit, squirrel or even a fox, she sternly told him to stop barking or she would put him back on the lead.

Eventually she had to carry out her threat as the dog would not keep quiet. Even once on the lead it still continued to bark and growl at either side of the path they were taking. It was at this very point that the lady reported that she saw movement all around her in

Old postcard of Caerleon, c. 1920s.

the undergrowth, accompanied by what appeared to be dark shapes flitting to and fro in the increasing gloom of twilight. Although whatever was out there was keeping out of range of the woman's direct line of vision, the dog was obviously being affected far more dramatically. He began to twitch, yelp and whimper as though being hit by a force or object invisible to the woman. Despite her understandable fright, the lady managed to gather her composure and she quickly hurried back to the car where her dog was soon back to his usual self. Following this somewhat unexpected and harrowing event, she did attempt to return to the woods with her dog, but from that day on he refused to go near the area where something clearly terrified him.

The next incident happened to an elderly gentleman out for a leisurely stroll along almost the same route as the previous woman and her dog. This particular episode happened on a cold winter's afternoon in full daylight. He had no sooner left the church when he heard what he described as heavy footsteps on the track behind him. He turned, expecting to see someone following him, maybe in a hurry to get past him, but when he looked the track behind was completely empty. Putting it down to an overactive imagination he continued into the wood only to hear the heavy footfall behind him yet again and, as you can probably guess, on turning to get sight of the owner of these footsteps, there was nobody to be seen. At that stage he claims he was intrigued more than scared, and in a strange way fascinated as to what was causing this unusual and perplexing phenomenon. In order to test the unseen perpetrator he tried stopping and starting several times, and even walking on the undergrowth on the side of the path. However, each time he restarted his walk the footsteps soon followed.

Little did he know that soon events would change and his initial curiosity would turn to fear! The first indication that something unpleasant was about to happen was an icy cold blast of air on the nape of his neck. Although it was a cold day, he described the effect as being more like someone blowing an icy breath very close to his skin. Next he described an enveloping blanket of what he thought was a menacing energy around him, accompanied by a marked difficulty with his own breathing. Although he described himself as a non-practising Christian, it was one of those moments when it seemed time to get some help from any source possible, and he began to pray out loud. The result was an immediate reaction as the unseen force that had him in its grip abated. He turned around, still scared, and out of the corner of his eye he saw what he described as a dark swirling shape disappearing rapidly into the trees and, as a result, the negative feeling appeared to depart with it. Still very shaky and unsettled, he walked briskly onward to Caerleon and to the bus that would take him home, the very place he felt the need to be now. Although his wife might have wondered many times why he refused to go for future walks in those particular woods, it was some considerable time before he felt able to share his tale.

As already mentioned, a waymarked path goes through these woods and a few years ago a young female hiker was taking this route to Caerleon. Unlike the others mentioned earlier, she had successfully traversed most of the wood and was now on the outer edge overlooking the stunning Usk Valley, with her next destination clearly in view. It was a lovely clear and bright day so she decided to sit on a fallen tree close by and eat her lunch. Whether it was a result of the hearty meal she had just consumed or tiredness overtaking her suddenly, as it sometimes does, she began to feel drowsy and had to really struggle to keep herself awake. It was at this point that she claimed she felt a very definite prod in her back and, on turning, she could not determine what may have caused it. Thinking it was some sort of internal spasm linked to walking, eating and tiredness, she continued viewing the vista. That was until she felt a further two prods in very quick succession! She was now convinced that there was some kind of supernatural force playing games with her. Whatever the entity or entities were that had prodded her, the unusual and quite annoying phenomenon continued for some fifteen minutes, always going for her back no matter which direction she turned.

Although she felt a bit on the foolish side, the young lady started to strike up a conversation with her unseen tormentors, asking for them to reveal themselves to her. Although she could not locate where it was coming from, suddenly faint noises like high-pitched giggling drifted across the air towards her. Again asking for them to reveal themselves, she suddenly caught a fleeting glimpse of what appeared to be two very small children disappearing into the wood at a rapid rate. Now very excited, with all earlier signs of sleepiness long since gone, she chased them in the general direction they had taken and ended up in a small clearing that had several large clumps of mushrooms scattered around it. She was of the age to immediately recognise them as 'liberty caps', probably better known as magic mushrooms. The effects of liberty caps are similar to a mild dose of the drug LSD and can vary greatly depending on the mood, situation and expectation of the user. Had she then somehow accidentally ingested spores of these mushrooms in the air during her lunch that resulted in the hallucinations that she had just experienced? Or had she perhaps had a genuine encounter with the fairy-folk of this place that had decided, for whatever reason, to play with her and reveal themselves briefly?

Although the explanations to all these unusual experiences may never become clear, it does seem very likely that these woods would be a very interesting location to study the paranormal.